The Blue-Cliff Record

Other Books by David Hinton

WRITING

Wild Earth, Wild Mind

China Root

Awakened Cosmos

Desert

The Wilds of Poetry

Existence: A Story

Hunger Mountain

Fossil Sky

TRANSLATION

The Way of Ch'an: Essential Texts of the Original Tradition

The Selected Poems of Tu Fu: Expanded and Newly Translated

No-Gate Gateway

I Ching: The Book of Change

The Late Poems of Wang An-shih

The Four Chinese Classics

Classical Chinese Poetry: An Anthology

The Selected Poems of Wang Wei

The Mountain Poems of Meng Hao-jan

Mountain Home: The Wilderness Poetry of Ancient China

The Mountain Poems of Hsieh Ling-yün

Tao Te Ching

The Selected Poems of Po Chü-i

The Analects

Mencius

Chuang Tzu: The Inner Chapters

The Late Poems of Meng Chiao

The Selected Poems of Li Po

The Selected Poems of T'ao Ch'ien

The Selected Poems of Tu Fu

THE
BLUE-CLIFF
RECORD

TRANSLATED BY

David Hinton

SHAMBHALA

Shambhala Publications, Inc.
2129 13th Street
Boulder, Colorado 80302
www.shambhala.com

Cover art: Shitao. Winding Path Up Mountainside.
China, 1694. Ink and color on paper. 27.94 x 22.22 cm.
Los Angeles County Museum of Art, 60.29.1h. www.lacma.org. Public Domain.
Cover design: Kate Huber-Parker
Interior design: Steve Dyer

9 8 7 6 5 4 3 2 1

FIRST EDITION
Printed in the United States of America

Shambhala Publications makes every effort
to print on acid-free, recycled paper.
Shambhala Publications is distributed worldwide by
Penguin Random House, Inc., and its subsidiaries.

Library of Congress Cataloging-in-Publication Data
Names: Yuanwu, 1063–1135, author. | Hinton, David, 1954– translator.
Title: The Blue-Cliff Record / David Hinton.
Other titles: Bi yan lu. English
Description: Boulder: Shambhala Publications, 2024. | Includes index.
Identifiers: LCCN 2023028111 | ISBN 9781645472704 (trade paperback)
Subjects: LCSH: Koan.
Classification: LCC BQ9289 .Y8213 2024 | DDC 294.3/443—dc23/eng/20231023
LC record available at https://lccn.loc.gov/2023028111

Contents

Introduction

THERE ARE NO ANSWERS, only depths. If there were an anthem for *The Blue-Cliff Record* and Ch'an more broadly, this might be it: there are no answers, only depths. But the depths—oh my, the depths are wondrous indeed! For those depths are beyond the words and explanations and understanding that answers normally entail—and there, anything and anywhere is the answer: willow seed-fluff swarming sunlit through afternoon skies, hummingbird probing blue-violet iris blossoms veined gold, someone answering a knock at the courtyard gate:

> Boundless wind and moon are the eye within the eye,
> limitless heaven and earth the lamp beyond the lamp.

> A million homes amid dark willows and lit blossoms:
> knock at any gate anywhere, and someone will answer.

This poem was considered a kind of preface to *The Blue-Cliff Record*, and indeed *The Blue-Cliff Record* is all about dismantling the answers one might expect to find in the teachings of some sage-master, about opening those depths that are one's own inherent nature. But learning how *The Blue-Cliff Record* works its magic beyond words, how to inhabit those depths beyond explanations—naturally, that requires a few words and explanations.

The Ch'an written tradition cultivated those depths over centuries, primarily in prose works by and about Ch'an masters, records of their lives and teachings. These records contain a great deal of conventional explanatory teaching, which is necessary to prepare students for Ch'an's wordless insight, its boundless depths. That direct insight is conveyed in the more literary dimension of those records: poetry, which is perfectly suited to the quick, deep insights of Ch'an, and storytelling typified by poetic distillation: enigmatic sayings and wild antics intended to upend reason and tease mind past the limitations of logical thought. These are performative, rather than explanatory—enacting insight, rather than talking about it. As such, they operate with poetic wildness and immediacy, instead of the usual discursive explanation. In this, they come as close as language can to those depths of Ch'an insight that lie outside words and teaching.

Ch'an teachers began drawing especially revealing moments from the records of earlier teachers, moments that distill the essential insights of Ch'an, and using them as teaching tools. These scraps of story came to be known as *kung-an* (公案, now widely known in its Japanese pronunciation: *koan*). *Kung-an* means a "law-court case," or more literally a "public case," and it was adopted to the Ch'an situation for a number of reasons. First, a *kung-an* presents a factual situation that needs to be understood accurately, like a court case—understood, however, at a level that precedes thought and analysis. Second, each *kung-an* represents a kind of precedent to which practitioners can refer. And finally, masters originally conducted *kung-an* training in "public," when the entire monastic community was gathered together. Hence the translation adopted here: "sangha-case" (*sangha* meaning "a Buddhist community").

Eventually, in tenth-century Sung Dynasty China, teachers began gathering these sangha-cases into collections used for training students. Three of these collections established themselves as the enduring classics, perennially employed over the centuries in China, then Japan, and on into Zen practice around the world today: *The Blue-Cliff Record* (ca. 1040 C.E.), *The Carefree-Ease Record* (ca. 1145), and *No-Gate Gateway* (1228). Such sangha-case collections are now generally treated by most teachers as mere collections of stories that provide an occasion for teaching. But in fact, they are masterpieces of classical Chinese literature, carefully constructed literary/philosophical texts designed to create—in and of themselves and without further explanation—a direct and immediate literary experience in the reader: the experience of awakening's wordless depths. In this, they are the culmination of Ch'an literary creation: a new and unique and profound literary form that combines zany storytelling with poetry and philosophical prose. Indeed, a sangha-case, containing the barest minimum of explanation, represents the most fully-realized written vehicle of Ch'an's "separate transmission outside all teaching."

This is typical of the Chinese philosophical tradition, where the seminal classics are all literary in nature—poetry and storytelling replete with interesting characters engaged in revealing conversation and events. For philosophy in ancient China was all about immediate experiential wisdom, rather than the abstract truths that occupy the Western tradition. And so, the world we enter in Ch'an literature is a community not of religious acolytes, but of philosophers exploring the deep nature of things together, and in a way that is experientially transforming.

The Blue-Cliff Record (碧巖錄) is the earliest of Ch'an's classic sangha-case collections. It established the form employed by collections that followed: the sangha-cases themselves supplemented with commentary. This form extends a tradition wherein classic texts included commentary that was considered an integral part of the text and a major philosophical genre in its own right, a tradition stretching all the way back to the beginning: the *I Ching*, China's first book, is virtually all "commentary."

In *The Blue-Cliff Record*, this structure divides neatly into two levels—a primary text and a secondary text—written by two different Ch'an masters. (This structure repeats exactly in *The Carefree-Ease Record*, and with one variation in *No-Gate Gateway*.) The primary text was written by Snow-Chute Mountain (Hsüeh Tou: 980–1052). It includes, first, the sangha-case itself, a scrap of story that Snow-Chute selected from the Ch'an tradition and retold with revisions that suited his literary purposes—most often radical distillation that highlights the story's essence. And second, the *gatha* (sutra-poem), a poetic "commentary" that provides an additional layer of insight. These function as direct teaching itself, as close to the immediate experience of wordless insight as we can get in language. This primary text contained one hundred chapters, each including a sangha-case and a *gatha*. It was known as *Snow-Chute Mountain's Gathas on the Ancients* (ca. 1040), and it was widely-influential.

The secondary text came eighty-five years later, when a Ch'an master named Awake-Entire (Yüan Wu: 1062–1135) used Snow-Chute's collection as a teaching text, giving lectures on each of the chapters. Awake-Entire's students took careful notes, which were eventually compiled and shaped into an extensive commentary on Snow-Chute's primary text. Although there is some direct teaching here, it mostly operates as secondary expli-cation. The compilation of these two texts became *The Blue-Cliff Record* (1125), named after the site where Awake-Entire taught.

Here we see a clear example of the conflict between Ch'an as direct mind-to-mind transmission outside of teaching and answers (primary text) and the natural belief that understanding comes through explan-atory teaching (secondary text). This conflict between direct word-less transmission and explanatory teaching is a problematic running all through the Ch'an tradition—not only because explanation precludes direct insight, but also because explanation is inevitably necessary as preparation for that wordless awakening, and in any case it serves institu-tional Ch'an's need for teaching programs, etc. One of the most famous flash-points in this conflict occurred when Awake-Entire's successor, Prajna-Vast (Ta Hui: 1089–1163), forcefully insisted that Ch'an awakening only comes through direct non-verbal insight, that eloquent explanation is a hindrance because it encourages students to rely on conceptual un-derstanding. Awake-Entire's commentary provides a classic example of eloquent explanation: it is massive, many times larger than the original text, drowning the original in explication. And in a dramatic act of direct Ch'an teaching in the sangha-case spirit, Prajna-Vast destroyed the orig-inal edition of Awake-Entire's *Blue-Cliff Record* and burned the wooden printing-blocks. He thereby overthrew his own teacher and forced stu-dents to encounter the direct teaching in Snow-Chute Mountain's orig-inal collection of sangha-cases and poems, rather than the secondary explanation that defies wild Ch'an's wordless spirit.[1]

Keeping faith with Ch'an as direct transmission, this translation pres-ents only Snow-Chute Mountain's original collection of sangha-cases and their companion *gathas*. *The Blue-Cliff Record* title is retained because it is so well-known to Western readers.

—————

Sangha-case collections like *The Blue-Cliff Record* are the culmination of Ch'an's historical development, because they incorporate and assume all of the insights and strategies that Ch'an had developed over the centu-ries. Once those insights and strategies are familiar, the seeming paradox of sangha-cases becomes approachable. And to understand the insights of Ch'an's direct transmission outside of words and explanations, to open ourselves to it here in *The Blue-Cliff Record*'s dynamic teaching, we must first understand the conceptual framework within which it operates.[2]

That framework is a constellation of concepts that form an ontology/ cosmology that was taken for granted in ancient China by Ch'an practitioners and indeed by all artist-intellectuals. These concepts appear, therefore, in texts like *The Blue-Cliff Record* without explanation. The Key Terms appendix at the end of this book (pp. 213–26.) defines those foundational concepts and can be read straight through as a short summary of Ch'an's conceptual world. That conceptual world is described more fully in my *China Root*. And the development of that framework through the millennia of proto-Ch'an and Ch'an texts in China is traced in my *The Way of Ch'an*. Those two books serve as the most complete introduction to *The Blue-Cliff Record*. In any case, once that framework is understood, the seeming paradox of sangha-cases becomes approachable. And the *gathas* become perfect and sufficient "commentary" on the sangha-cases: concise and insightful and challenging in much the same way as the sangha-cases themselves. Hence, a "commentary," but also a continuation of the direct insight enacted by the sangha-cases.

Ch'an's native philosophical world extends back over two millennia prior to *The Blue-Cliff Record*'s appearance, originating in the seminal Taoist texts: *I Ching*, *Tao Te Ching*, and *Chuang Tzu*. Taoist thought is best described as a spiritual ecology, the central concept of which is Tao, or Way. *Tao* originally meant "way," as in "pathway" or "roadway," a meaning it has kept. But Lao Tzu and Chuang Tzu, the original Taoist thinkers, redefined it as a generative cosmological process, an ontological path *Way* by which things come into existence, evolve through their lives, and then go out of existence, only to be transformed and reemerge in a new form. To understand Tao, we must approach it at its deepest ontological and cosmological levels, where it might be described as an "existence-tissue" that can be divided provisionally into two aspects: Absence (無) and Presence (有), concepts that represent the fundamental substrate of Ch'an practice.

Presence is simply the empirical universe, which the ancients described as the ten thousand things in constant transformation; and Absence is the generative tissue from which this ever-changing realm of Presence perpetually emerges. Or more properly, Absence is the existence-tissue seen not as ten thousand distinct forms, but as a single undifferentiated tissue that is boundlessly generative—the source of those ten thousand individual things. Way can be understood as the generative process through which all things arise and pass away as Absence burgeons forth into the great transformation of Presence. This is simply an ontological description of natural process, and it is perhaps most immediately manifest in the seasonal cycle: the pregnant emptiness of Absence in winter, Presence's burgeoning forth in spring, the fullness of its flourishing in summer, and its dying back into Absence in autumn.

Taoist dwelling as integral to Tao at the deepest level is Ch'an's primary concern; and as we will see, the wilderness cosmology of Absence and Presence is central to Ch'an practice. Absence (無: *wu*) is the more foundational of the two terms, and it is the basis of Ch'an practice. One appellation for the Ch'an school was 宗門, meaning most simply "ancestral gate" or "gate of the ancestors," hence a school of thought or practice handed down from the ancestors, wherein "gate" suggests both "household entered through a courtyard gate" (as in traditional Chinese dwellings) and "an entrance-way to insight." But more fundamentally, 宗門 means "source-ancestral gate," suggesting Ch'an is the gate into the source-ancestral. This source-ancestral is nothing other than 無: Absence, the ancestral ontological/cosmological source. And inhabiting this source-ancestral as home-ground is indeed the essence of Ch'an's two primary practices: meditation and sangha-case practice.

In bare philosophical outline, meditation begins with the practice of sitting quietly, attending to the rise and fall of breath, and watching thoughts similarly rise and fall, appearing and disappearing in a field of silent emptiness.[3] From this attention to thought's movement comes meditation's first revelation: that we are not, as a matter of observable fact, our thoughts and memories. That is, we are not that center of identity we assume ourselves to be in our day-to-day lives, that identity-center defining us as fundamentally separate from the empirical Cosmos. Instead, we are an empty awareness that can watch identity rehearsing itself in thoughts and memories relentlessly coming and going. Suddenly, and in a radical way, Ch'an's demolition of concepts and assumptions has begun. And it continues as meditation practice deepens.

With experience, the movement of thought during meditation slows enough that we notice each thought emerging from a kind of emptiness, evolving through its transformations, and finally disappearing back into that emptiness. Here we find the process of thoughts appearing and disappearing manifests Taoism's generative cosmology, reveals it there within the mind. And with this comes the realization that the cosmology of Absence and Presence defines consciousness too, where thoughts are forms of Presence emerging from and vanishing back into source-ancestral Absence, exactly as the ten thousand things of the empirical world do. That is, consciousness is part of the same cosmological tissue as the empirical world, with thoughts emerging from the same generative emptiness as the ten thousand things.

Eventually those thoughts fall silent, and we inhabit consciousness empty of all content. That is, we inhabit the most fundamental nature of consciousness itself, known in Ch'an parlance as *empty-mind* or *no-mind*. This is mind as 無, as source-ancestral—for as we have seen, that emptiness is the source of thoughts. This is to inhabit source-ancestral 無 as home-ground—dwelling that is, as we will see, crucial to sangha-case practice.

Indeed, 無 is the heart of sangha-case practice.[4] It contains a double meaning that Ch'an often exploits to great philosophical effect: in addition to "Absence," it also means "no/not." This double meaning informs a concept that explains the essence of sangha-case practice: *wu-wei* (無為). *Wu-wei* means "not acting," in the sense of acting without the identity-center self, or acting with an empty and therefore wild mind. This selfless action is the movement of the Cosmos, so *wu-wei* means action integral to the Cosmos's spontaneous burgeoning forth, action *as* the Cosmos. In fact, it means acting as the very source-ancestral of the Cosmos, for in addition to "not-acting," *wu-wei* means "Absence-acting." Hence, *wu-wei* action as action directly from, or indeed, *as* the generative ontological source-ancestral. And so, again, there is no *answer* in any conceptual sense, only the *depth* of this *wu-wei* dwelling.

Success in a sangha-case encounter always involves responding with this *wu-wei* spontaneity, action that lies outside any logical analysis. And sangha-case training pushes the student toward that goal with enigmatic utterances and outbursts and antics. The correct response in a sangha-case encounter is whatever thought or action emerges spontaneously from that silent emptiness cultivated in meditation practice, the generative emptiness of *wu*-mind (no-mind or Absence-mind), where the logical construction of thoughts has not yet begun. When Ch'an teachers examined students, they looked for students who moved in a direct and single-minded way—forceful, without self-doubt or hesitation—for those were students who had mastered *wu-wei*. This is radical self-reliance, trusting oneself rather than teachers and their words. And more radical still: it was *wu-wei* at the most profound level—"Absence-action," improvisational action in which one moves as the generative source, as the Cosmos unfurling its possibilities. And in this, it is cultivation of the sage dwelling that defines Ch'an enlightenment, dwelling heart and mind as an organic part of Tao's great transformation of things.

Such *wu-wei* responses take two forms—spoken words or physical action—and they exemplify the Ch'an of "wild words and wooly actions." When a sangha-case plays out in words, it grows directly out of the understanding of *wu-wei* gained in meditation. Rather than the calculating machinery of an isolated self, an insightful response emerges with selfless spontaneity from the empty origin-tissue: thought as Tao unfurling its transformations, or as "Absence-acting" (in contrast to the conventional idea of enlightenment as the perfection of thoughtless and tranquil emptiness). As physical action, an insightful response is selfless action as integral to the unfurling Cosmos, action moving with the dynamic energy of the Cosmos. Either way, words or actions, sangha-cases are not about explaining enlightened understanding; they are about *enacting* it.

The Blue-Cliff Record appears to be a series of teaching encounters in which we expect teachers to impart understanding and insight to students: answers. However, as an extension of meditation practice, sangha-cases always strive to dismantle thought and analysis, understanding and insight and even teaching itself, revealing that there are no answers, only the depths of empty-mind (no-mind or Absence-mind). But it doesn't end there. Each chapter is an encounter involving a number of individuals: the characters within the sangha-case; Snow-Chute Mountain commenting on the sangha-case in his *gatha*; and finally, the reader. In this encounter, it is usually unclear where the locus of insight lies: the apparent teacher is often undermined, outwitted by the student or someone else. Then Snow-Chute Mountain inevitably challenges, ridicules, thinks beyond the sangha-case's teacher. This deconstruction is reflected in the forms of Snow-Chute's *gathas*. Classical Chinese poems generally have very regular forms: notably lines of uniform length—usually five or seven words—arranged in couplets. Snow-Chute generally violates this form in his *gathas*, which usually contain lines of wildly varying lengths—a radical literary act that gives a formal representation of the demolition going on. This can be seen in the translations, where line lengths replicate lengths in the original: not numbers of words, but relative length on the page.

Finally, those demolition strategies suggest that in our reading of the chapter, we the readers are ourselves meant to overthrow both the sangha-case teachers and Snow-Chute himself, opening for ourselves those wordless depths. This assertion of thoroughgoing self-reliance represents one of Ch'an's most fundamental principles: that we are in our inherent nature always already enlightened, and that only by overthrowing teachers and their teachings (answers) can we realize this enlightenment (depths). It is a welcome reassurance, especially for women, in a tradition that seems on the surface to be defined by an oppressive male hierarchy.

Once we overthrow those teachers, we can walk out into the world finding the answer everywhere and nowhere, as in *The Blue-Cliff Record's* preface poem:

無	邊	風	月	眼	中	眼
no/ Absence	boundary	wind	moon	eye	middle	eye

不	盡	乾	坤	燈	外	燈
no	end	Heaven	Earth	lamp	outside	lamp

柳	暗	花	明	千	萬	戶
willow	dark	blossom	bright	thousand	ten thousand	house

敲	門	處	處	有	人	應
knock	gate	place	place	there is	person	answer

Boundless wind and moon are the eye within the eye,
limitless heaven and earth the lamp beyond the lamp.

A million homes amid dark willows and lit blossoms:
knock at any gate anywhere, and someone will answer.

The lamp in line 2 is radiant empty-mind, absolute depth passed from teacher to student directly in a "separate transmission outside all teaching," the very essence of Ch'an traced in the great Ch'an history (written in the same era as *The Blue-Cliff Record*): the *Lamp-Transmission Record* (傳燈錄). Here there is no answer at all, nothing to teach or learn, only radiant empty-mind depths that are the very nature of consciousness itself, the original-nature all sentient beings share. From this comes Bodhidharma's seminal proposal that we are always already awakened, that we only need to recognize that original empty-mind nature: "seeing original-nature, you become Buddha" (see Key Terms, p. 224).

Identifying that lamp with "heaven and earth," the poem invests radiant empty-mind with cosmological dimensions. Heaven and earth normally appear as 天地, meaning simply the Cosmos. But here in the poem they appear in an alternate formulation that emphasizes the cosmological dimensions of the Cosmos: 乾坤. The Taoist Cosmos was described as ch'i (氣): a single tissue generative through and through, the matter and energy of the Cosmos seen together as a single breath-force surging through its perpetual transformations. 氣 was divided into two fundamental principles whose dynamic interaction generates the process of change: *yang* (male, light, heat) and *yin* (female, dark, cold). The term 乾坤 emphasizes heaven and earth as the grandest cosmological manifestations of *yang* and *yin*: Heaven as the active generative force of the Cosmos and Earth as the receptive generative force. In this, the universe was conceived as a dynamic and perpetual interpenetration of *yang* and *yin*, a *ch'i*-tissue. And returning to the poem, we find the lamp of radiant empty-mind at the deepest cosmological/ontological levels identified with this magisterial heaven and earth, this *ch'i*-tissue Cosmos: the very definition of awakening.

In the radiant lamp of empty-mind, the act of perception magically becomes a spiritual practice in which the opening of consciousness is a mirror allowing no distinction between inside and outside. Identity becomes whatever sight fills eye and mind, becomes all of existence itself: the poem's "boundless wind and moon" landscape, its "limitless heaven and earth" Cosmos. In this mirroring, landscape becomes the "eye within the eye," and heaven and earth the "lamp beyond the lamp." This may be the beginning and end of Ch'an: no ideas, no stories, no certainties, no questions and no answers, no seeking—just empty-mind become the wordless thusness of things in and of themselves. This sheer thusness of the ten thousand things is the wordless teaching that returns consciousness to empty mirror-mind depths. A sangha-case is meant to replace words and ideas with the sheer thusness of things, the master's wild and surprising antics startling the student's mind out of analytical thought and into the immediate empty-mind experience of that thusness. Those empty-mind depths are described in an alternate reading of the first couplet that is allowed by its wide-open grammar:

The eye within the eye is boundless amid wind and moon,
the lamp beyond the lamp limitless amid heaven and earth.

But there's more. A second reading lurks playfully beneath the poem's surface, for its first word is 無 (wu: "no/Absence"), with its rich double meaning. Here, 無邊 means not only the more straightforward reading "no + boundary/border" (also recommended by the parallel grammatical structure of the first two lines), but also "Absence + boundary/border." Hence: "In the borderlands of Absence, the eye within the eye." And so, we return to meditation and its revelation that our original empty-mind nature is itself Absence, that generative "source-ancestral" from which thoughts arise. And as 無 precedes word and explanation and understanding, it is not an answer. It is pure depth, wondrous depth.

In his seminal "Regarding the Source-Ancestral," the first distinctively Ch'an text, Hsieh Ling-yün (385–433 C.E.) calls those depths of empty-mind "the tranquil mirror, all mystery and shadow." He goes on to say that for enlightenment one must "become Absence and mirror the whole." In this poem introducing *The Blue-Cliff Record*, the answer comes not from a sage Ch'an master in some majestic monastery tucked away amid breathtaking mountains, but from anyone at all. And that answer is the sheer thusness of things—wordless and inexplicable, no answer at all—returning you to those empty Absence-mind depths. It could be a Ch'an master's antics, or just as easily the householder answering your knock at the gate: in Ch'an, the *gate* is always the entrance-way to awakening, and here it is clear that any gate will do. And turning away from that house after your knock has been answered, you set out into the wind-scoured and moonlit expanses of all heaven and earth, the mirror-deep depths of sight opening those expanses of thusness inside you, lighting that radiant lamp. And in the midst of all those depths, what is there to enlighten?

THE
BLUE-CLIFF
RECORD

1

Bodhidharma Vast-Expanse Absence

Southlands Emperor War-True[5] asked the Grand-Master Bodhidharma: "What is the first principle of sage reality?"

"Vast-expanse no-sage Absence,"[6] replied Bodhidharma.

"Then who is this facing me here?"

"No idea."

The emperor couldn't mirror Bodhidharma's mind. So, Bodhidharma crossed the Yangtze and made his way to the kingdom of Origin-Height.

Later, the emperor asked Master Remembrance-Treasure about this, and Remembrance-Treasure said: "Now do you know who that was?"

"No idea."

"It was Avalokitesvara, the World-Gaze bodhisattva, transmitter of Buddha's mind-imprint."

The emperor was full of regret, and told someone to go invite Bodhidharma back. But Master Remembrance-Treasure said: "Don't bother. Even if you send the whole kingdom to plead with him, he'll never come back."

GATHA

Sage reality all vast-expanse, how
could it ever be clear and evident?

An emperor asks *Who is this facing
me here?* He later answers *No idea.*

And so, Bodhidharma slipped across the river
one night, escaping thickets of thorn-bramble.

Even if the whole kingdom were sent, he'd never come,
and brooding a thousand, ten thousand forevers is empty.

Just don't brood over it,
then clear wind sweeps around this world boundlessly,

and a great master looking out in all directions,
wondering if there are any patriarch masters to be found,

you say to yourself: "Yes?
Well then, send them here to wash this old monk's feet."

2

Visitation-Land Inhabit Tao

Instructing the assembled sangha, Visitation-Land said: *It isn't hard to inhabit Tao's Way. Simply stop picking and choosing.*[7] The moment even a first word or thought appears—that's already picking and choosing, already the clarity of understanding. This old monk doesn't abide in the clarity of understanding. But it's still the treasure you cherish, isn't it?"

A monk interrupted and asked: "If not the clarity of understanding, what is your cherished treasure?"

"I really don't know," replied Land.

"But if you don't know, Master, how can you say that you don't abide in the clarity of understanding?"

"Asking is itself the realization," replied Land. "Just ask, then bow reverently and leave."

GATHA

It isn't hard to inhabit Tao's Way,
but words begin, thoughts begin,

and in one lies the seed of many,
in two the nature of all before it.

At the edge of heaven, sunrises and moonsets,
at the fence, deep mountains and cold streams:

when the skull stops making distinctions, how can joy survive?
It's just the dragon-cry of an age-torn tree, faint but never gone.

Hard, hard: the clarity of
understanding, picking and choosing. It's how we see ourselves.

3

Grand-Master Sudden-Horse Was Unwell

Grand-Master Sudden-Horse Way-Entire was unwell. The abbot asked: "How are you feeling these days, Master?"

"Sun-face Buddha. Moon-face Buddha."

GATHA

Sun-face Buddha. Moon-face Buddha.
What primal sage-emperor compares?[8]

After twenty bitter years gone raiding the black dragon's
secret lair, he seized the Buddha-truth pearl. All for you,[9]

and now he's offering it.
Enlighten-eyed patchrobe monks, don't take this lightly!

4

Heart-Sight Pilgrim Sack

When he was a monk traveling, Heart-Sight Mountain visited River-Act Mountain. He walked straight into the Dharma Hall, pilgrim sack tucked under his arm. There, stalking east to west and west to east, he surveyed the scene and bellowed: "Absence! Absence!" Then he left.

> *Commenting on this, Snow-Chute Mountain said: "Broke it open!"*

He got as far as the courtyard gates, then reconsidered: "Even so, not harebrained and wild-ass enough!"

So he composed himself, assuming a solemn majesty, then went back inside to face River-Act Mountain properly. River-Act sat perfectly still. Clarity snatched River-Act's sitting cushion out from under him and held it up, then called out: "O Master!"

River-Act hesitated, then grabbed his Buddha-whisk.[10]

"*KHO-AAA!*" shouted Clarity. Then he billowed his sleeves out in a swirl and left.

> *Commenting on this, Snow-Chute Mountain said: "Broke it open!"*

Clarity turned his back to the Dharma Hall, put on his straw sandals, and walked off.

That night, River-Act Mountain asked the head monk: "The monk who just arrived—where is he now?"

"He turned his back to the Dharma Hall, put on his straw sandals, and set out," replied the head monk. "He's gone."

"One day, he'll climb an isolate peak somewhere, build a thatch shrine-hut on the summit. And so, he'll go on laughing at Buddhas and scolding patriarchs."

> *Commenting on this, Snow-Chute Mountain said: "Just piling frost on snow!"*

GATHA

Broke it open once,
Broke it open twice,
then piling frost on snow: risky crag and quite a tumble.

It's like General Fleet-Horse caught in the enemy camp:
how many get away like him, their lives whole and free?

But scurrying around
won't win liberation,

and sitting in a thatch hut on the summit of some isolate peak:
AI-OO!

5

Snow-Peak Rice Grain

Instructing the assembled sangha, Snow-Peak Mountain said: "The whole vast expanse of this world: I pick it up in my fingertips, and it's tiny as a rice grain. I toss it right here in front of your faces, but you buckets of lacquer still don't understand. Beat the drum, summon everyone to come look, look!"

GATHA

Mind's ox-head demons vanish
and horse-head demons appear,
but the Sixth Patriarch's mind-mirror is free of dust.[11]

Beat the drum, come and look: if you still don't see,
how can spring's hundred blossoms bloom for you?

6

Cloud-Gate Marvelous Days

Cloud-Gate Mountain announced: "I'm not asking you about the days before a full moon. But the days after a full moon: say something about that, quick."

Answering for the sangha, he said: "One day after another, and they're all marvelous days!"

GATHA

Give up primal unity, and find
the wild multiplicity of things
above and below in every direction. There's nothing like it:

to amble along in regal ease, tracing the sound of streamwater,
to gaze far and wide, soaring free along paths of birds in flight!

Rich confusions of grasses
among hazy veils of mist:

there, you're emptiness-born amid cliffwall paths, wildflower
profusions, and a mere snap of the fingers erases old *sunyata*.[12]

Now, don't move an inch!
One inch, and I'll give you thirty blows!

7

Prajna-Leap Asks Buddha

A monk named Prajna-Leap asked Dharma-Eye: "I wonder if the master would explain what Buddha is?"

"You are yourself Prajna-Leap," answered Dharma-Eye.

GATHA

In river country, spring wind still, a mountain partridge deep
among wildflowers cries out. Three-Cascade Gorge: it's there[13]

amid towering waves that fish are transformed into dragons,
but dullards just keep dipping out buckets of pondwater night.

8

Kingfisher-Cliff Mountain Eyelids

Instructing the assembled sangha at the end of summer session, Kingfisher-Cliff Mountain said: "I've been here all summer for you, my friends. I've talked and talked. Now, look closely at this Kingfisher-Cliff: am I blinded by eyelids pinched closed?"[14]

"It takes an empty mind to be a thief," observed Prosper-Nurture Mountain.

"Revealed," quipped Reward-Perpetua Mountain.

"Gateway," declared Cloud-Gate Mountain.[15]

GATHA

In Kingfisher-Cliff's teaching,
a thousand ages facing Absence.

That one-word *gateway* is perfect
crime, all the money stolen away,

and who fathoms Prosper-Nurture
buffeted on storm-swells of life?

Kingfisher-Cliff yammering on:
it's theft of a flawless white-jade

amulet. How many can tell reality
from the reality our words conjure?

But Reward-Perpetua understands
just what eyes wide open reveal!

9

Visitation-Land Four Gates

A monk asked Visitation-Land: "What is Visitation-Land?"
"East gate. West gate. South gate. North gate."

GATHA

Words revealing the loom-of-origins, splitting your head open,
sight a diamond-flame sword clearing away all trace of dust:

those gates face you directly—east and west, south and north—
but attacking with a hammer, you'll never break through them.

10

Placid-Land Stolen Emptiness

Placid-Land asked a monk: "Where in all this wordless Absence-tissue have you just come from?"

"*KHO-AAA!*" shouted the monk.

"One shout. Okay, I'll accept one shout."

"*KHO-AAA!*"

"Three or four shouts like that, and then what?"

The monk fell silent.

Land struck him a blow, and said: "You oaf! Your head's full of stolen emptiness!"

GATHA

Two or three *KHO-AAA!* shouts to reveal you
fathom the loom-of-origins all transformation?

If that's what they call riding the tiger's head,
they're oafs, both of them, reckless and blind.

Who reckless and blind?
I come carrying all beneath heaven. I hold it out for you. Take a look!

11

Yellow-Bitterroot's
Nibbling at Stale Wine-Dregs

Instructing the assembled sangha, Yellow-Bitterroot Mountain said: "You're oafs like all the rest, nibbling at stale wine-dregs. If you keep up your traveling-pilgrim nonsense, where will you find anything like this very today? Don't you know there isn't a single Ch'an teacher anywhere in the whole empire?"

A monk leapt forward to interrupt: "What!? But there are people everywhere nurturing disciples and leading sanghas. So what are they revealing?"

"I didn't say there's no Ch'an, just that there are no teachers."

GATHA

Aloof and cool, Yellow-Bitteroot thought nothing of himself,
seas all around where he meditated with dragons and snakes.

He struck Emperor Center-Vast three blows. The emperor
took it lightly, no idea he was playing with claws and fangs.

12

Fathom Mountain's *Flax. Three Pounds.*

A monk asked Master Fathom Mountain: "What is Buddha?"
"Flax. Three pounds."

GATHA

Gold-crow sun fleet,
jade-rabbit moon fast:
answering like that, you never feel the slightest blow. Inhabit

this loom-of-origins unfurling, and you see Fathom Mountain.
If not, you're turtles lame and blind gone into empty valleys.

And wildflower blossoms blooming brocade-blossom blooms,
southern bamboo vast—O—vast northern forests: it makes me

think of Reward-Perpetua Mountain at his teacher's funeral
telling monks that it was a time not for tears, but for laughter.

CHAA!

13

Open-Hand Ridge's
Source-Ancestral Teaching

A monk asked Open-Hand Ridge: "What is the source-ancestral teaching in Patriarch Flood-Deva Risen's torrent of words[16]?"

"Gathering snow in a silver bowl."

GATHA

Sage old Open-Hand Ridge:
there's truly no one like him
for explaining it all so clearly: *Gathering snow in a silver bowl*!

The ninety-six ancient schools should understand for themselves:
if they don't, they should ask moon drifting above the sky's edge.

Flood-Deva Risen's teaching,
Flood-Deva Risen's teaching
hoists crimson banners of victory, and there a crystalline wind rises.[17]

14

Cloud-Gate's *Talk Primal-Unity Directly Faced*

A monk asked Cloud-Gate Mountain: "What was the actual teaching of Buddha himself?"

"Talk that is primal-unity directly faced," replied Cloud-Gate.

GATHA

Talk primal-unity directly faced:
he's perfectly alone and distant
wedging that handle into an iron hammer-head with no hole.

Under the Gate-Drift Tree shading this universe, he laughs on
and on, and just last night broke off the black dragon's horns.[18]

Wondrous, how wondrous
old man Cloud-Gate turning horn into a primal-unity handle!

15

Cloud-Gate's *Talk Primal-Unity*
All Topsy-Turvy

A monk asked Cloud-Gate Mountain: "If it isn't the loom-of-origins instance-by-instance unfurling before my eyes, and it isn't occurrence moment-by-moment simply appearing of itself before my eyes—then what is it?"

"Talk that is primal-unity all topsy-turvy."

GATHA

Words primal-unity all topsy-turvy:
he cleaves the primal-unity season,
offering your farewell at death and welcome at birth.

Buddha's eighty-four thousand disciples failed to see,[19]
and only thirty-three patriarchs entered the tiger cave.[20]

Wondrous, how wondrous
its confusions of frenzied flickering: a moon in water.

16

Clarity-Mirror Out In

A monk asked Clarity-Mirror Mountain: "I'm pecking out of this shell. Can you give me some help, please, and start pecking in?"

"You're alive, aren't you?" replied Clarity-Mirror.

"If I'm not, people I meet must think me a strange sort of thing."

"You're still an oaf lost in weeds and grasses."

GATHA

That old Buddha possessed such style,
and it stripped that monk's display bare.

Chick and hen never know each other,
but someone's pecking both out and in.

Pecking in awakens,
but he's still inside his shell—

then the next blow is struck!
Patchrobe monks everywhere call it profound. What good's that?

17

Incense-Forest's *Sitting Long in Meditation Tedious Work*

A monk asked Incense-Forest: "What is the *ch'i*-weave[21] mind Bodhidharma brought from the West?"

"Sitting long in meditation like him: it's just tedious work."[22]

GATHA

One chance, two, this life's thousand ten-thousand chances:
just tear those blinders away and throw off your cargo bags!

Searching left and right, following others around: that's why
Mongrol Purple-Calm struck Iron-Grinder that mighty blow.

18

Prajna-Devotion Shrine-Tower

Emperor Source-Ancestral Awe asked Nation-Teacher Prajna-Devotion: "Your hundred-year life is ending. Afterwards, what can I do for you?"

"Build this old monk a shrine-tower stitched from Absence," replied Prajna-Devotion.

"What style of shrine-tower?" asked the emperor.

Prajna-Devotion was silent for some time, then said: "You don't understand."

"No, I don't."

"I've entrusted the dharma to a monk named Source Tiger-Glare. He knows all about these things. Summon him and ask."

After Prajna-Devotion returned to the great transformation of things, the emperor summoned Source Tiger-Glare and asked him to explain. Source said:

South of Appearance River and north of Deep-Lake River:

> Commenting on this, Snow-Chute Mountain said: "A single hand wastes no sound."

there at the center, you find enough gold for the whole country.

> Commenting on this, Snow-Chute Mountain said: "Mountain-raw travel-staff." [23]

Where trees cast Absence-shadow, the accord-whole boat drifts:

> Commenting on this, Snow-Chute Mountain said: "Quiet seas, clear rivers."

it's a crystalline hall of meditation. You recognize no one there.

> Commenting on this, Snow-Chute Mountain said: "Offered up in open hands."

GATHA

Shrine-tower stitched from Absence:
it's difficult to see. There's no black-
dragon coiled around the Buddha-truth pearl in a lake deep and pure.[24]

Ridgelines rising layer above layer,
shadow deepening pool within pool:
there, it's been revealed for a thousand, ten thousand forevers gone.

19

Million-Million One Finger

Whenever a question was posed, Master Million-Million simply raised one finger.

GATHA

I say this loud and clear: I love old Million-Million deeply.
But who are we when all seed-time breath-space is empty[25]

home? How could anyone dangle driftwood into vast seas
and rescue blind-turtle adepts in billowing swells of night?[26]

20

Dragon-Fang Meditation Clapper

When he was a monk traveling, Dragon-Fang Mountain asked Kingfisher Shadowed-Emergence:[27] "What is the *ch'i*-weave mind Bodhidharma brought from the West?"

"Pass me that clapper to announce meditation," said Shadowed-Emergence.

Dragon-Fang passed the wooden clapper to Shadowed-Emergence, who swung it and struck Fang a blow.

"You can strike me all you want," hissed Dragon-Fang. "But there's still no *ch'i*-weave mind for Bodhidharma to bring from the West."

Traveling years later, after his awakening under Fathom Mountain, Dragon-Fang asked Purport Dark-Enigma: "What is the *ch'i*-weave mind Bodhidharma brought from the West?"

"Pass me that meditation cushion," replied Dark-Enigma.

Dragon-Fang passed the cushion to Dark-Enigma, who swung it and struck Fang a blow.

"You can strike me all you want," cackled Dragon-Fang. "But there's still no *ch'i*-weave mind for Bodhidharma to bring from the West."

GATHA

1

Dragon-Fang Mountain's blind dragon haunts dead
water. How can ancient wind ripple that back to life?

Meditation clapper or cushion: if you can't use them,
just pass them over to Master Thatch-Hut Mountain.[28]

2

Pass them to old Thatch-Hut, and you're free, no more
meditation promising you the lamp patriarchs transmit.

Just face evening clouds drifting uneasily home, distant
ridgeline rising above blue ridgeline boundlessly away.

21

Wisdom-Gate Lotus Blossom

A monk asked Wisdom-Gate Mountain: "Before a lotus blossom[29] rises above the water, what is it?"

"Lotus blossom," replied Wisdom-Gate.

"And after it rises above the water—what then?"

"Waterlily leaf."

GATHA

Lotus blossom, waterlily leaf: now you understand, right?
Risen above water: how can that be anything like before?

Trekking north and south of the river asking this and that
old master: it's just one tricky fox-question after another.

22

Snow-Peak Mountain's *Turtle-Nose Viper*

Instructing the assembled sangha, Snow-Peak Mountain said: "There's a turtle-nose viper on South Mountain.[30] All of you, you really need to go take a close and careful look."

Reward-Perpetua Mountain said: "Here in this Dharma Hall, how many have lost their lives to that snake's venom, lost even their place in the grand unfurling of things?"

Another monk asked Dark-Enigma-Sands Mountain about it, and Dark-Enigma-Sands said: "That's just like Reward-Perpetua. It's a start, but not how I do things."

"How would you reveal this?" asked the monk.

"Why bother with South Mountain?"

Suddenly, Cloud-Gate Mountain threw his travel-staff down in front of Snow-Peak Mountain, and leapt back in fear.[31]

GATHA

No one scales Snow-Peak Mountain's towering cliffwalls
unless they can charm that snake and carry it in their hands.

Reward-Perpetua and Dark-Enigma just couldn't manage it,
and how many have lost life and fate to that snake's venom?

But old Cloud-Gate understood,
unleashed wild origins, knowing
you never find it searching south and north, east and west.

Suddenly unsheathing his travel-staff clear out to the head,
he threw it down before Snow-Peak, mouth vast and open,

wide open—O—vast and quick, a lightning strike slicing
eyelids away, opening eyes. And yet, no one quite saw it,[32]

just like now: viper hiding here on Snow-Chute Mountain,
pilgrims coming to perfect those principles and practices,

and my own towering shout: *KHO-AAA!*
Look out! There at your feet!

23

Prosper-Nurture Wandering Mountains

When they were students, Prosper-Nurture Mountain and Reward-Perpetua Mountain were out wandering mountains. Prosper-Nurture pointed and said: "Look! Right here! This is the very summit of Wondrous-Mystery Peak!"

"Yes, yes. But saying so . . . that's really too bad," said Reward-Perpetua.

> Commenting on this, Snow-Chute Mountain said: "Here today, what's the point of wandering mountains with oafs like that?"

> Commenting further, Snow-Chute Mountain said: "There are few, even in a hundred thousand years, who don't try to speak of Absence."

Later, someone told Clarity-Mirror Mountain what happened, and Clarity-Mirror said: "If it hadn't been Reward-Perpetua, the countryside would be littered everywhere with skulls."

GATHA

Lavish with wild-origin grass, isolate Wondrous-Mystery
Peak offered clear-eyed illumination—but who's looking?

And it isn't Reward-Perpetua's precise explanation. Skulls
litter the ground everywhere. How many understand that?

24

Iron-Grinder's *Lookout-Terrace Mountain*

When Iron-Grinder stopped at River-Act Mountain, Mountain said: "Venerable Water-Buffalo, you've come!"

"Tomorrow, our vast sangha gathers on Lookout-Terrace Mountain for the seclusion-fast,"[33] she announced. "It's only a thousand miles away. Are you going?"

River-Act Mountain lay down and stretched out for a nap.

Iron-Grinder went on her way.

GATHA

Riding her iron horse, she enters the double-walled city
to proclaim tranquil clarity throughout our six kingdoms.

Gold crop in hand, she invites travelers to return home.
It's deep night. Who sets out with her on the long road?

25

Shrine-Hut Master Lotus-Blossom
Peak's *Walking-Stick*

Shrine-hut master Lotus-Blossom Peak raised his travel-staff and instructed the assembled sangha: "When sage ancients came into this here-within, why didn't they stay?"

The sangha remained silent, so he answered for them: "It couldn't offer them the power of life's Buddha-Way road ahead."

Then his instruction continued: "Then what is utter enlightenment?"

Again answering for the sangha, he said: "To sling a walking-stick over your shoulder and, leaving people without looking back, to wander deep into a thousand, ten thousand peaks."

GATHA

The dust of this world glutting our eyes and ears, who
wouldn't wander into a thousand, ten thousand peaks?

Blossoms fall, creeks flow: it's boundless and beyond.
Slice lids away, open eyes wide: where is it you'll go?

26

Hundred-Elder Mountain's
Grand and Wondrous Affair

A monk asked Hundred-Elder Mountain: "What is the grand and won-drous affair?"

"To sit alone here on Valiant-Vast Mountain," replied Hundred-Elder.

The monk bowed. Hundred-Elder struck him a blow.

GATHA

Sudden-Horse's foal gallops far and wide across patriarch fields.[34]
Our Ch'an gate changes, paths differ: some explain, some mystify.[35]

Lightning flash, flint spark: live the loom-of-origins as it comes.
What a laugh: that numbskull come grabbing the tiger's whiskers!

27

Cloud-Gate's *Potency Laid Bare to a Golden Wind*

A monk asked Cloud-Gate Mountain: "What is it when year-end trees wither and leaves tumble away?"

"That potency[36] shaping the actualization of things, potency frost-bitten and laid bare to a golden wind."

GATHA

Question and answer both all
source-ancestral, Cloud-Gate

sends one triple-insight arrow
piercing empty-sky distances:

vast wildlands—O—vast and bitter wind moaning, moaning;
boundless skies—O—boundless and thin rain hissing, hissing.

Can't you see Bodhidharma in this, a traveler never returning
home, meditating at Rare-Shrine Forest all those
years serene into death among Bear-Ear's assembly of peaks?

28

Wellspring-South Mountain's
Not This Mind Buddha

Wellspring-South Mountain and Hundred-Elder Mountain were talking through things. Hundred-Elder said: "Have sages from the beginning all possessed a dharma they could not talk about, not explain to anyone?"

"Yes," replied Wellspring-South.

"How is it revealed, this dharma that cannot be talked about?"

"Not this mind," proclaimed Wellspring. "Not this Buddha. And not this world of things."

"You're talking about it!" countered Hundred-Elder.

"I am this thusness I am, simply doing what I do. How do you reveal that dharma?"

"I still haven't achieved insight vast and whole. How could I understand what can and cannot be talked about?" confided Hundred-Elder.

"No idea," replied Wellspring.

"Hah! So I've talked this to death for you!" exulted Hundred-Elder.

GATHA

Patriarchs and Buddhas never explain anything to anyone.
Patchrobe monks keep chasing neck-and-neck after them,

even though things parade through mind's radiant mirror,
always new. They look south to see the Northern Dipper.

Its handle may hang low,
but where could they ask
its secrets? Our original-face has no mouth talking, talking.[37]

29

Tumble-Vast Kalpa-Fire

A monk asked Tumble-Vast Mountain: "When the kalpa-fire's[38] perfect understanding burns this thousand-Buddha-realm Cosmos down into ruins, will this unthought here-right-now also be burned down into ruins?"

"Down into ruins," replied Tumble-Vast.

"Will even thusness itself vanish away with it?"

"Away with it."

GATHA

There in the midst of blazing kalpa-fires, the moment he asks,
that patchrobe monk swings the heavy gateway to awakening

closed. *Away with it:* how wondrous that precept. And yet, he
searched on here and there alone, ten thousand hell-bent miles.

30

Visitation-Land

A monk asked Visitation-Land: "They say you met Wellspring-South Mountain face-to-face. Is that true?[39]
 "They grow huge radishes in Wellspring-South country."

GATHA

They grow huge radishes in Wellspring-South country:
you patchrobe monks everywhere think it's an answer,

insight whole all the way from ancient to future times.
How can you even tell white egrets from black crows?

Thief! Thief!
Old Visitation-Land has snatched your original-face clean away!⁴⁰

31

Flax-Canyon Sangha-Staff

Still an advanced monk, Flax-Canyon Mountain took up his sangha-staff and went to see Manifest-Revere. He circled around Revere's meditation cushion three times, shook his staff once, then stood looming there before him.

"Yes, right! Right!" said Revere.

Commenting on this, Snow-Chute Mountain said: "Wrong."

Later, Flax-Canyon Mountain went to see Wellspring-South Mountain. He circled around Wellspring's meditation cushion three times, shook his sangha-staff once, then stood looming there before him.

"No, not right! Not right!" said Wellspring.

Commenting on this, Snow-Chute Mountain said: "Wrong again."

The moment pregnant, Flax-Canyon asked: "Manifest-Revere said *Yes, right!* Master. Why then do you say *No, not right?*"

"Manifest-Revere may have said *Yes, right!* but you weren't right at all. This is how storm-gales tumble you finally into ruins."

GATHA

This wrong and then that wrong:
never approving or disapproving,

waves rest calm on the four seas
and lakes feed the hundred rivers.

Take that old staff to the twelve windswept gates meditation
opens, each with its own path of desolate and silent emptiness:

without that emptiness,
you're just searching for medicine when there's no sickness.

32

Purport Dark-Enigma and the Buddha-Dharma's Vast *Ch'i*-Weave Insight

When he was head-monk, Samadhi-Still[41] asked Purport Dark-Enigma: "What is the Buddha-dharma's vast *ch'i*-weave insight?"

Dark-Enigma leapt from his meditation seat, grabbed hold of Samadhi-Still and gave him a single slap, then pushed him away.

Samadhi-Still froze and just stood there.

"Head-monk Samadhi-Still," called out another monk, "why don't you bow?"

Samadhi-Still thereupon bowed reverently, and suddenly had a great awakening.

GATHA

Yellow-Bitteroot taught Purport the decisive slice exhausting[42]
each loom-of-origins moment. Who needs carefree ease then?

Opening a way through, the Yellow River god raised his hand
and simply split ten million Flourish Mountain ridges asunder.

33

Prosper-Sustain's *Origin-Mind Circle*

Minister Held-Array went to see Prosper-Sustain Mountain. When Prosper saw him approaching, he drew an origin-mind circle[43] in the dirt.

"Coming here, I am this thusness I am, simply doing what I do," said Held-Array, "no instantaneous awakening revealed. Why force the issue by drawing this circle?"

At that, Prosper-Sustain stepped back inside the gates of his abbot's house.

> *Commenting on this, Snow-Chute Mountain said: "Held-Array possesses the Buddha-deep eye's clarity whole."*

GATHA

Circle of Buddha-truth pearl exquisitely round, clittering jade-pure:[44]
loading it on horses, on camels and mules and iron ships, pilgrims

may wander mountains and oceans carefree. But pry it half-open,
and you can hook that vast turtle bearing up this three-peak world.

Commenting on this, Snow-Chute Mountain said: "Patchrobe monks
throughout all beneath heaven try to leap free, try and fail."

34

Reliance Mountain's *Five-Elders Peaks*

Reliance Mountain asked a monk: "Where in all this wordless Absence-tissue have you just come from?"

"From the Thatch-Hut Mountains," replied the monk.

"And did you walk up among Five-Elder Peaks there?"

"No, I didn't."

"My friend," exclaimed Reliance, "you didn't walk among those Thatch-Hut Mountains at all!"

When he heard this story half a century later, Cloud-Gate Mountain observed: "All that small-talk lost in the weeds: it was just Reliance Mountain's compassion for a monk."

GATHA

Leave weeds and you enter weeds:
who can get free of our searching?

White cloud swells and billows up,
red sun flares steady and blazes on:

look left, and everything's flawless;
turn right, and it's already gone old.

Haven't you seen
how master Cold Mountain set out when he was still young:[45]

ten years on a mountain without ever returning,
he couldn't even remember the way he'd come.

35

Manjusri's *Three-Deep Three-Shadowed-Earth Samadhi*

Sutra-Kill Manjusri,[46] regal teacher of Buddhas, asked Absence-Belong: "Where in all this wordless Absence-tissue have you just come from?"

"The south," replied Absence-Belong.

"And how is the Buddha-dharma faring there?"

"In this age of dharma's demise, almost no one there honors the laws and precepts."

"How many sanghas are there?" continued Manjusri.

"Maybe three or five hundred."

Then Absence-Belong asked Manjusri: "And how is the Buddha-dharma faring here?"

"Commoners and sages live together. Dragons and snakes tangle together."

"How many sanghas are there?"

"Three-deep three-shadowed-earth *samadhi* before me. Three-deep three-shadowed-earth *samadhi* behind me."

GATHA

A thousand coiled peaks stretched writhing indigo-jade away
there, who could accuse Manjusri of small-talk? It's laughable

asking like that: *How many sanghas on Lucid-Chill Mountain?*
Three-deep three-shadowed-earth *samadhi* before and behind.

36

Perpetua-Sands Wandering Mountains

Perpetua-Sands went wandering in the mountains one day. When he returned, just as he reached the gate, the head monk asked: "Where did you go, Master?"

"I went wandering in the mountains," replied Perpetua-Sands.

"And where did you return?"

"I set out following wildflower scents," said Perpetua-Sands, "and I came back following fallen blossoms."

"Such is the *ch'i*-weave mind of spring," offered the head monk.

"It's even better than autumn frost dripping on lotus blossoms," responded Perpetua-Sands.

> *Commenting on this, Snow-Chute Mountain said: "Gratitude spoken in answer."*

GATHA

This vast earth is exquisitely free of dust:
how can anyone's eyes not be wide open?

So he set out following wildflower scents
and came back following fallen blossoms.

Bone-thin crane perching in cold treetops,
crazed gibbon calling on ancient terraces:

Perpetua's *ch'i*-weave mind boundlessly!
AI-OO!

37

Swirl-Roam Mountain's
Three Realms Absence No-Dharma

Swirl-Roam[47] Mountain announced: "Throughout its three realms,[48] this everyday *samsara*[49] universe is everywhere Absence no-dharma.[50] So where could you ever find mind?"

GATHA

Samsara is everywhere Absence-
dharma, so where could you find

mind? Hidden amid white clouds,
cascading streams play their *ch'in*[51]

music: one song, two songs, and still no one understands.
Rain sweeps across a pond at night—water autumn-deep.

38

Wind-Source Mountain's *Iron-Ox Totem*

At the magistrate's pavilion in Altar-Evince Land, Wind-Source Mountain ascended his teaching platform in the Dharma Hall and said: "The mind-seal of patriarchs is like those huge iron-ox totems people build along rivers to ward off flooding. Lift it away quickly, and the seal remains clearly stamped. Leave it long, and the seal smears into ruins. And what if you neither lift it nor leave it? Is it the seal itself, or is it not?"

At that, the venerable Black-Deer Scarp stepped forward and said: "I already possess that iron-ox totem. Who needs your seal stamped all over it?"

"I'm always fishing for great whales in these floodwaters so crystalline and vast," countered Wind-Source. "How did I catch this frog plopping around in muddy sand?"

Scarp just stood there, baffled.

"*KHO-AAA!*" shouted Wind-Source. "A venerable monk, and nothing to say?"

Scarp still paused, considering.

Swinging his abbot-staff, Wind-Source struck him a blow. Then he said: "Have you completely forgotten what we're talking about? Show me something!"

Scarp opened his mouth to speak, but Wind-Source struck him another blow.

Then the magistrate spoke up: "The dharma-law of Buddha and the dharma-law of governance—they're no different."

"What inner-pattern Way have you seen?" asked Wind-Source.

"If you don't correct when correction is needed, chaos follows."

Wind-Source descended from his seat.

GATHA

He lifted Black-Deer Scarp atop that iron-ox totem, but how
answer lance-and-shield attacks all dark-enigma three deep?

Rivers pass imperial cities returning to source-ancestral seas:
one shout and they flow back toward mountains: *KHO-AAA!*

39

Cloud-Gate

A monk asked Cloud-Gate Mountain: "What is pure and clear dharma-nature?"

"Peony hedge," replied Cloud-Gate.

"Ahh—thusness-of-itself. And if I tear that hedge out, what then?"

"Buddha-lion with golden fur."[52]

GATHA

Peony hedge: hey,
don't piss around!
Weight's marked on the scale—O—the scale, not on what's weighed out.

Ahh—thusness-of-itself:
bottomless, utter enigma!
Buddha-lion with golden fur: all you in our vast household, look closely!

40

Wellspring-South Mountain's *Very Blossom*

Once, when he was talking with Wellspring-South Mountain, the high minister Solar-Extent Continual said: "Dharma-master Sangha-Fundament[53] claimed *This heaven-and-earth Cosmos and I share the same root. The ten thousand things and I share the same original potency.*[54] How absolutely wondrous that is!"

Pointing to a blossom in the courtyard, Wellspring-South said to Solar-Extent: "These days, people see this very blossom as if it were some kind of dream-mirage."

GATHA

In awakened perception, there's no longer this me and that other,
no longer a mirror holding rivers and mountains in its deep gaze.

Frost-laden skies, moon sinking low—now, midway into night,
who shares reflections shimmering cold in crystalline lakewater?

41

Visitation-Land

Visitation-Land asked Dice-Thrown Mountain: "After dying utterly to this world, mind exquisitely vacant, the Great Death—how is it when a person comes back to life?"

"You needn't travel by night," replied Dice-Thrown, "to arrive in the thrown enlightenment of morning."

GATHA

Eyes wide open here in this life: that too is the Great Death.
If you want healing medicine, why examine revered masters?

Even sage Buddha said he himself never arrived. Occurrence
numberless as the sands: who can scatter it like garden seed?

42

Shelter-Dragon Layman's *Wondrous Snow*

When Shelter-Dragon Layman left Medicine Mountain, Medicine sent ten visiting pilgrims with him to offer farewell at the gate. Shelter-Dragon pointed into the sky filled with snow and said: "This wondrous snow, flake after flurried flake: it isn't falling anywhere else!"

"Where *are* they falling?" asked a pilgrim named Entire.

Shelter-Dragon struck him a blow.

"Awfully wise-ass for a layman," said Entire.

"This is what you are? And you call yourself a Ch'an pilgrim?" countered Shelter-Dragon. "Even the king of hell wouldn't give you a place to stay!"

"And you, layman? You think you're better? You think you're revealing something here?"

Shelter struck the pilgrim another blow, and said: "Your eyes are blind when they look. Your mouth is mute when it speaks."

> Commenting on this, Snow-Chute Mountain said: "At the first word,
> I'd grab a snowball and strike a blow!"

GATHA

Snowball strike a blow!
Snowball strike a blow!
Old Shelter-Dragon never found that gateway the loom-of-origins opens.

Of all the gods above and humans below, no one ever knows themselves,
but in that isolate place within eye and ear, we live always free and clear,

perfectly free and clear.
Even Bodhidharma the blue-eyed barbarian, even he couldn't explain it.

43

Fathom Mountain's *No Cold and No Heat*

A monk asked Fathom Mountain: "How can I avoid life's summer heat and death's winter cold?"

"Why not go to a place where there's no cold and no heat?" replied Fathom.

"What kind of place is that?"

"Where cold is so cold it destroys you, and hot is so hot it destroys you."

GATHA

Reaching down, a master's helping-hand is an eighty-thousand-foot cliff.
Existence-tissue whole or as the different things we know: must you see

it utterly? In ancient palaces of crystal radiant with moonlit illumination,
there's a terribly clever dog chasing rabbits up the staircase of emptiness.

44

Field-Grain Mountain's
Awakening Drum Struck a Blow

Handing insight down to the assembled sangha, Field-Grain Mountain said: "Devotion to study is called *listening*. Liberation from study is called *intimacy*. And passing beyond both of those, that is to pass so far beyond that you become the wild thusness of things."

A monk stepped forward and asked: "What is passing so far beyond that you become the wild thusness of things?"

"Awakening drum struck a blow!"

"What is it, in actuality, this wild thusness of things?"

"Awakening drum struck a blow!" repeated Field-Grain.

"This mind this Buddha: I'm done asking about that. But what is neither mind nor Buddha?"

"Awakening drum struck a blow!"

"When someone already enlightened arrives, how do you welcome them?"

"Awakening drum struck a blow!"

GATHA

We pestle-grind
and dirt-stir, but
powerful as a twenty-ton crossbow, the loom-of-origins keeps unfurling

occurrence itself. Facing the sangha, old Snow-Peak Mountain rolled out
three balls.[55] How is that like Field-Grain's *awakening drum struck a blow*?

Here's the secret:
let tangles alone.
This life's sweetness is simply sweet—O—and its bitterness simply bitter.

45

Visitation-Land Plaincloth Shirt

A monk asked Visitation-Land: "The ten thousand dharmas return to primal-unity. And what does primal-unity return to?"

"When I was in Green-Azure Land," replied Visitation, "I made a plaincloth shirt. It weighed a whopping ten pounds!"

GATHA

The question leans in close, but that ancient awl-sharp sage cuts deep, and who can understand his *shirt a whopping ten pounds*?

Right now, every scrap of cargo tossed overboard on West Lake, I'm sailing light and free on a clear wind. Who'll ever share this?

46

Clarity-Mirror Mountain's
Clatter of Falling Rain

Clarity-Mirror Mountain asked a monk: "What's that sound outside?"

"The clatter of falling rain," answered the monk.

"People have turned themselves upside-down," mused Clarity-Mirror. "Following after things, they've lost themselves."

"What about you, Master?"

"I never lose myself anymore," replied Clarity.

"What does it really mean, to never lose yourself?" asked the monk.

"When you've just begun, it seems easy. But once you get free, it's impossible to talk about."

GATHA

Empty Dharma Hall, the clatter of falling rain,
sage-master facing a monk, answer impossible:

if you call that entering the stream of everyday
life, it's the same as ever: you don't understand

anything, not anything. In all that
torrential rain, North Mountain and South Mountain switch places!

47

Cloud-Gate's *Six Depths of Consciousness Can't Take It All In*

A monk asked Cloud-Gate Mountain: "What is dharma-nature?"[56]

"The six depths of consciousness[57] can't take it all in," replied Cloud-Gate.

GATHA

One, two, three, four, five, six: dharma-nature is plenitude
too immeasurable even for Bodhidharma, that blue-eyed barbarian.

They're lying when they say he entrusted it to the Second Patriarch.
Others claim he went, shrouded in robes of mystery, back to India,

India far away and vast. Who could ever find him there? Luckily,
dharma-nature's here all night long facing Snow-Chute Mountain.

48

Governor Anyone's *Tea Ceremony*

Governor Anyone came for the tea ceremony at Reward-Beckon Monastery. Assisting Lumen-Beckon Mountain, head-monk Lucid-Still fumbled the teapot and tipped it over. Seeing this, the governor asked: "What's underneath the tea-stove?"

"There's a stove-spirit down there," taunted Lucid-Still.

"Then how could you be so clumsy?"

"Lofty official for a thousand days," countered Lucid-Still, "lose it all in a single morning."

The governor billowed his sleeves out in a swirl, and left.

"Head-monk Lucid-Still," said Lumen-Beckon, "you've long taken your meals here in the monastery, and still you go out wandering wildlands beyond the river, strike fire-scorched tree stumps enlightening blow after blow?"

"You think you're revealing something here, wise one?"

"Cripples piss and shit, do the best they can."

> Commenting on this, Snow-Chute Mountain said: "That's when I would have kicked over the tea-stove!"

GATHA

Anyone asks like flawless wind. Answering that pure
moment in the unfurling loom-of-origins, Lucid-Still

hardly excelled. And Reward-Beckon, that half-blind
dragon: how sad that he never bared fangs and claws,

fangs and claws that unleash seething
cloud and lightning-flash. How often
can you wander upstream, returning home through that storm's waves?

49

Three-Sage Escaped Net

Three-Sage Mountain asked Snow-Peak Mountain: "A golden-scale fish escaped the net, and you still haven't said what it will eat."

"Once you've escaped that net, I'll tell you about it," replied Snow-Peak.

"Fifteen hundred students, grand master of the perfectly wise word, and not a word to say!?"

"This old monk somehow became an abbot, and that brings such tangles of trouble."

GATHA

A golden-scale fish escaped the net:
don't think water keeps it hemmed in!

Billowing heaven and sweeping earth,
fins heaving deep, huge tail thrashing,

it's a thousand-foot whale breaching through vast waves into flight,
into a lightning-flash searing and deafening, storm-gusts crystalline,

storm-gusts crystalline.
How many in all heavenly and peopled realms, how many understand?

50

Cloud-Gate Earth *Samadhi*

A monk asked Cloud-Gate Mountain: "What is the entrance every fleck of dust offers into three-shadowed-earth *samadhi*?"

Cloud-Gate replied: "Rice in the rice-bowl, water in the water-pail."

GATHA

Rice in the rice-bowl, water in the water-pail:
what can the twittering bird beaks of little masters ever teach

when Northern Dipper and Southern Star never change places,
and waves seething through heaven billow up from level earth?

Longing or not longing, abiding or not abiding,
we inherit all Buddha's wealth, but can't afford pants to wear.

51

Snow-Peak What's This

When Snow-Peak Mountain was living at the shrine-hut, two monks came to offer bows in reverence to him. When he saw them coming, Snow-Peak pushed the courtyard gate open, leaned out and said: "What's this?"

One of the monks said the same thing back: "What's this?"

Snow-Peak bowed slightly and went back inside.

Later, that monk went to visit Crag-Summit Mountain.

"Where have you just come from?" asked Crag-Summit.

"From Summits-Pass South."

"Did you visit Snow-Peak Mountain there?"

"Yes."

"What's he teaching people these days?"

The monk told Crag what happened, and Crag asked: "So, what did he say?"

"Nothing. He just bowed slightly and went back inside the shrine-hut."

"Ah, well. I've always regretted that, when I saw him, I didn't explain all the way beyond a last-ever utterance. If I had, no one in all beneath heaven could rival old Snow-Peak."

At the end of the summer session, the monk asked again about Snow-Peak, hoping to understand more deeply.

"Why didn't you ask the first time?" wondered Crag-Summit.

"I knew it wasn't easy, and I didn't want to pry."

"Snow-Peak and I share this one lineage, but we won't die in the same lineage. If you want to understand all the way beyond a last-ever utterance, it's simply *This! This right here!*"

GATHA

All the way beyond a last-ever utterance:
it was offered for you yourself. Mingle
illumination and darkness together, then you'll come to understand.

Sharing our one lineage, they know each other through and through;
but not dying in the same lineage, they're spectacular worlds apart,

spectacular worlds altogether far apart,
same as Buddha and Bodhidharma. Those two understood perfectly.

South, north, east, west: let's go home in all our separate directions
and together in depths of night, gaze at snow atop a thousand peaks.

52

Visitation-Land Stone Bridge

A monk said to Visitation-Land: "I've long heard talk about how Visitation-Land is a stone bridge. But now I've come, all I see is a little plank."

"Well, if all you see is a little plank," replied Land, "of course you don't see a stone bridge."

"What is this stone bridge?" asked the monk.

"Mules *cross-beyond* over it. Horses *cross-beyond* over it."[58]

GATHA

On isolate and dangerous peaks, climb higher. In seas of boundless awakening, hook that vast turtle bearing up this three-peak world.

Asked the same question about himself, old master Libation-Creek said *Arrow splitting air!* What a laugh: hard work, and for nothing.

53

Hundred-Elder Mountain's *Wild Ducks*

Grand-Master Sudden-Horse Way-Entire was out walking with his student Hundred-Elder Mountain. When they saw wild ducks flying over, the grand-master asked: "What is that?"

"Wild ducks," replied Hundred-Elder.

"Where have they gone?"

"They've flown away."

Grand-master Way-Entire pinched Hundred-Elder's nose and twisted hard. Hundred-Elder cried out in pain, and the grand-master said: "When did wild ducks ever fly away?"

GATHA

Those wild ducks understand
precisely where they've gone.
When Patriarch Way-Entire sees them, he speaks. When he stops,

things seen are part of us again—mountain cloud, ocean moon—
and we're back where we started: unable to fathom *flown away*.

Almost altogether flown away
and held exactly where you are:

it's Way! Way!

54

Cloud-Gate's *Two Hands Face-Up*

Cloud-Gate Mountain asked a monk: "Where in all this wordless Absence-tissue have you just come from?"

"Ch'an-Still West," replied the monk.

"What's Ch'an-Still West talking about these days?"

The monk held out his two hands face-up. Cloud-Gate struck him with an open palm, then the monk said: "Exactly what I was saying!"

Cloud-Gate thereupon held out his own two hands face-up. The monk said nothing. Cloud-Gate again struck him with an open palm.

GATHA

A tiger head-to-tail out stalking, stalking, he unfurls magisterial
winds howling bitter and cold all across the four hundred lands.

You say *I don't know that risky pass through impossible peaks*,
and the master says *Let go, just let go of realization and set out!*

55

Way-I Mountain's *Can't Tell, Can't Tell Way*

Way-I Mountain and his student Source-Gradual visited a mourning household to offer condolences. Source slapped the coffin and said: "Birth? Or death?"

"I can't tell birth, and I can't tell death," replied Way-I.

"Why not?" asked Source.

"Can't tell, can't tell Way."

On their journey home, Source stopped and said: "Right now, Master, quick: tell me! If you don't, I'll strike you a fierce blow!"

"If you strike me, you strike me," countered Way-I, "but if I tell you Way, I don't tell you Way."

At that, Source struck him a blow.

Eventually, Way-I returned to the great transformation of things. Source-Gradual went to visit Stone-Frost Mountain and told him what had happened. Frost said: "I can't tell birth, and I can't tell death."

"Why not?" demanded Source.

"Can't tell, can't tell Way."

Hearing those words, Source had an awakening.

Later, Source took a shovel into the Dharma Hall, where he stalked from east to west and west to east. Stone-Frost asked: "What are you doing?"

"Looking for the wordless bones of our dead teacher," explained Source.

"It's all vast waves billowing across boundless seas, white-foam swells flooding sky," said Frost, "so what dead teacher, what wordless bones could you be looking for?"

Commenting on this, Snow-Chute Mountain said: "Blue sky. Blue sky."

"It's the perfect practice to build strength."

A century later, Utter-Origin Confident said: "The wordless bones of our dead teacher: they're always everywhere here."

GATHA

Rabbits and horses with horns,
oxen and goats without horns;

not a hair's-breadth, not a wisp,
like mountains, like high peaks:

those wordless bones are still around today—everywhere, purest gold.
But it's all white-foam swells flooding sky, utterly nowhere to practice,

nowhere to practice.
And Bodhidharma went back home to India, one sandal, lost completely.[59]

56

Gold-Delight Mountain's *One Arrow-Tip Breaking Through Three Gateways*

A visiting pilgrim-monk named Deep-Still asked Gold-Delight Mountain: "What's it like, that moment when a single arrow-tip breaks through three gateways into awakening?"

"Send the gatekeeper out to look," replied Mountain.

"So that's it," said Deep-Still. "Now I see what needs to change in me."

"What are you waiting for?"

"A perfectly-aimed arrow reveals nothing of what it hits," countered Deep-Still, who turned to leave.

"Come here!" shouted Mountain.

Deep-Still looked back. Mountain grabbed hold of him and said: "That single arrow-tip breaking through three gateways: it abides in stillness, never moving. Let's see you launch that arrow at me."

Deep-Still hesitated, paused to consider.

Mountain struck him seven blows with a staff and said: "You oaf! You'll waste thirty years mulling this over!"

GATHA

Why not venture out yourself with that gatekeeper and take a look?
Serene monks launching arrows: what vast and reckless confusion!

Cling to the eye—O—the eye, and your ears grow deaf as dragons.
Give away the ear—O—the ear, and your eyes turn blind as drums.

A single arrow-tip breaking through three gateways: it's wondrous,
and afterwards, your path ahead is sheer clarity in all radiant detail!

Haven't you heard
what old Dark-Enigma-Sands taught—O—
for those ancient sages and elders, those patriarchs, ancestral sky is itself mind?

57

Visitation-Land's *Not Picking and Choosing*

A monk asked Visitation-Land: "You said *It isn't hard to inhabit Tao's Way. Simply stop picking and choosing.*[60] But what is *not picking and choosing*?"

"Of all those in heaven above and earth below, to honor and follow myself alone."

"That's still picking and choosing."

"You great bumpkin! Where's the picking and choosing?"

The monk was dumbfounded, speechless.

GATHA

Deep as ocean expanses,
solid as mountain heights,

old Visitation-Land is a storm-gale that gnats in empty sky struggle to defy,
an iron pillar that ants try to shake down into tumbled ruins.

Picking—O—choosing—O—
it's a rag-cloth drum of silence.

58

Visitation-Land's *Five Years Explain Clearly*

A monk asked Visitation-Land: "You said *It isn't hard to inhabit Tao's Way. Simply stop picking and choosing.* For people these days, isn't that just a narrow-minded pitfall?"

"I was asked that five years ago," replied Visitation-Land. "I've seen through it with utter clarity ever since, and I still can't explain it clearly."

GATHA

Buddha's elephant-call truth,
Buddha's lion-roar teaching:

it's all flavorless talk packing
throats full, silencing voices.

South, north, east and west—
crows simply fly, rabbits run.

59

Visitation-Land Inhabit Way

A monk asked Visitation-Land: "You said *It isn't hard to inhabit Tao's Way. Simply stop picking and choosing. The moment even a first word or thought appears—that's already picking and choosing.*[61] But then, how can you teach people, Master?"

"Why didn't you quote it clear through to the end?"

"That's all I remember."

"Alright. Here it is, the whole thing: *It isn't hard to inhabit Tao's Way. Simply stop picking and choosing.*"

GATHA

Water rains down never wetting it,
wind howls through never entering,

tiger stalking and dragon roaming,
ghost wailing, spirit weeping: who

knows what this Visitation-Land monster is, head three feet long?
Facing us without a word, he stands isolate and perfectly content.

60

Cloud-Gate Mountain's
Travel-Staff Become Dragon

Cloud-Gate Mountain raised his travel-staff[62] and instructed the assembled sangha: "This travel-staff has become a dragon. It's wolfed down all *yang* and *yin*, heaven and earth. Rivers and mountains, this vast land—where will you ever find all that now?"[63]

GATHA

A travel-staff wolfs down all *yang* and *yin*, heaven and earth.
Why yammer about peach blossoms drifting waves away where

fish climb Three-Cascade Gorge: lightning-struck becoming
dragons, no need[64]
to grasp for cloud and mist; or falling back down, beached, no
need to lose heart.

He raised his travel-staff:
did you understand or not?

It's simple: just wander life's lazy scatter, free and easy
and no more struggling at tangled threads of confusion.

Seventy-two blows with his staff would let them off way too easy
and a hundred-fifty blows wouldn't set them free. So, the master

suddenly grabbed his staff and bounded off the teaching platform,
and that panicked sangha—they fled out into a sun-drenched land.

61

Wind-Source Dust Mote

Teaching the assembled sangha, Wind-Source Mountain said: "We established a first dust mote, gave it a name that separated it out from the existence-tissue, and before long there was a whole nation run rampant. If we give up that dust mote, the nation vanishes away."

> *Holding up his travel-staff before the assembled sangha, Snow-Chute Mountain said: "Can any of you patchrobe monks live Wind-Source Mountain's life, die Wind-Source Mountain's death?"*

GATHA

Sage teachings won't ease worry furrowing farmland-elder brows:
they want the nation established on a strong and noble foundation.

If it were, we'd be rid of scheming ministers and savage generals.
Ten-thousand-mile crystalline wind: such clarity knows only itself.

62

Cloud-Gate's *Utter Mystery Everywhere in This Wide World, This Mountain of Forms*

Instructing the assembled sangha, Cloud-Gate Mountain said: "Within all heaven and earth, this seed-time breath-space home,[65] right at the very center, there is a perfect jewel. Its utter mystery shines everywhere in this wide world, this mountain of forms. Take a dragon-weave lantern into the Buddha Hall; then bring this whole three-gate monastery of mountain liberation, and toss it into the flame."

GATHA

See!? See there!?
Who is it lazing out along ancient shorelines with a fishing-pole?

Clouds drift away, one by one,
and water brims vast into flood.
There, in reed blossoms of moonlit radiance, you can see yourself.

63

Wellspring-South Chopped Kitten

One day at Wellspring-South Mountain, monks from the eastern and western Sangha Halls were arguing over a kitten. When Wellspring-South Mountain saw this, he grabbed the kitten and held it up, saying: "If someone can say it all, say Way realized utterly, I won't chop it in two!"

No one answered. Wellspring chopped the kitten into two halves!

GATHA

Eastern and western Sangha Halls, all those Ch'an pretenders:
blissful, no idea what to do, they just kick up smoke and dust,

waiting for old Wellspring-South to grant the complete insight.
One blade delivering two halves: it was a try, however flawed.

64

Visitation-Land Straw Sandal

Wellspring-South Mountain told his head-monk Visitation-Land what happened and asked his opinion. Visitation-Land suddenly took off his straw sandal and balanced it on his head, then walked out.

"If you'd been there," Wellspring called out after him, "that kitten would have been saved!"

GATHA

To bring the sangha-case full-circle, he asked Visitation-Land.
They were in Peace-Perpetua, wandering the city all idleness,[66]

and Land balanced a sandal on his head, Absence unknowable.
Later he returned home to the mountain, settled into sage ease.

65

Someone Outside Asked Buddha

Someone outside our Buddha-Way sangha asked Buddha: "I'm not asking about Presence or what can be said. And I'm not asking about Absence or what can't be said."

The World-Honored-One was silent for a long time.

"World-Honored-One," the outsider said in praise and admiration, "vast in compassion, vast in sympathy—you've opened the clouds of my delusion, showing me how to enter inside Buddha-Way itself."

After the outsider left, Ananda asked Buddha: "What did that outsider experience? What did he realize that made him speak of entering inside Buddha-Way itself?"

"He's like a world-renowned horse," replied the World-Honored-One. "If it glimpses even the shadow of a whip, it's off and running!"

GATHA

Loom-of-origins wheels around without turning, turning
Absence and Presence at once, delusion and awakening.

Suddenly standing in this body, mind's brilliant mirror[67]
gazes out. And it sees distinctions like beautiful and ugly,
distinctions like beautiful and ugly—O—there, clouds of delusion begin.

Gates of compassion can never arise amid the tawdry dust of this world,
hence that world-renowned horse glimpsing even the shadow of a whip

runs a thousand miles chasing wind. And when it's called, it comes back,
it comes back and calls out, showing the three-deep *samadhi* way ahead.

66

Crag-Summit's *Collect Yellow-Nest's Celestial Sword*

Crag-Summit Mountain asked a monk where he'd just come from, and the monk answered: "From the capital, Peace-Perpetua."

"After the rebellion was crushed, did you collect Yellow-Nest's celestial sword?"[68]

"Yes, I got it," replied the monk.

Crag-Summit stretched his neck out right up close to the monk and shouted: "OW!"

"Your head is tumbling away!" cried the monk.

Crag-Summit roared with glorious laughter.

Later, the monk went to see Snow-Peak Mountain, and Snow-Peak asked: "Where have you just come from?"

"From Crag-Summit Mountain."

"What did he say to you?"

The monk told Snow-Peak what had happened. Snow-Peak struck him thirty blows with his staff and drove him out.

GATHA

Sword collected after Yellow-Nest's rebellion was crushed,
roaring with such glorious laughter: Crag-Summit sees it all.

That monk got off easy, thirty blows with a mountain staff:
to seize a liberating moment is to lose a liberating moment.

67

Bodhisattva Touch-Origin
Explains the Sutra

Southlands Emperor War-True asked Bodhisattva Touch-Origin to explain the *Diamond Sutra*. Touch-Origin ascended the teaching platform in the imperial hall. Seated there, he picked up the lectern and gave it a fierce shake. He set it back down, then rose and descended from his seat. The emperor was startled, dumbfounded. Master Remembrance-Treasure asked: "Does your majesty understand?"

"No, not at all."

"The Bodhisattva just explained that sutra through and through."[69]

GATHA

Leaving his Double-Forest shrine, Touch-Origin offered himself.
In a southland kingdom, he stirred the tawdry dust of this world,

and if he hadn't shown Remembrance-Treasure such realization,
it would have been Bodhidharma fleeing through the night again.

68

Reliance Mountain Roars
with Glorious Laughter

When he was a monk traveling, Three-Sage Mountain visited Reliance Mountain. Reliance asked: "What is your name?"

"Reliance Mountain," replied Three-Sage.

"Aren't I Reliance Mountain?!" exclaimed Reliance.

"Then my name must be Three-Sage Mountain!"

At this, Reliance roared with glorious laughter.

GATHA

Gathering themselves and scattering away, source-ancestral
itself, they rode a tiger at origins. It demands utter realization,

but that laughter ends. Who knows where they went, caught
here in this wind opening grief through a thousand ages lost.

69

Wellspring-South Mountain's
Origin-Mind Circle

Wellspring-South Mountain, Source-Ancestral Return, and Flax-Canyon Mountain set out to visit Nation-Teacher Prajna-Devotion and pay homage with reverent bows. Along the way, Wellspring-South drew an origin-mind circle[70] in the dirt and said: "If you can say it all, say Way realized, I'll keep going."

Source-Ancestral Return sat down in the middle of the circle. Flax-Canyon curtsied.

"In that case, I'm not going anywhere," declared Wellspring-South.

"What kind of gadabout mind is that?" asked Source-Ancestral Return.

GATHA

Source-Ground's arrow circled around a huge tree
before killing that gibbon: a perfectly direct route.

Thousands try, tens of thousands try, but how many
hit the bull's-eye dead-on? And so, he called them,

summoned them back home. Twofold-Creek Road
leading to Prajna-Devotion: there, he just gave it up.

> Commenting further, Snow-Chute Mountain said:
> "But Twofold-Creek Road is level and smooth:
> so why give up the visit?"

70

Hundred-Elder Mountain's
Throat and Tongue, Mouth and Lips

River-Act Mountain, Five-Peak Mountain, and Cloud-Crag Mountain were senior monks under Hundred-Elder Mountain. One day, Hundred-Elder asked River-Act: "Forget about throat and tongue, give up mouth and lips—now, how will you reveal it all, how say Way realized?"

"Give up and let you do it, old man," replied River-Act.

"I'm not refusing to reveal your Way realized," countered Hundred-Elder, "but I'm afraid that if I do, I'll never have dharma descendants."

GATHA

Give up and let you do it, old man: and so it is,
a tiger grows horns and stalks out of those weed-ridden wastelands.

Spring ends on the ten islands of sage immortals. Blossoms wither
and crumble. Across vast forests of coral, brilliant sunlight blazes.

71

Hundred-Elder Throat Tongue

Hundred-Elder Mountain asked Five-Peak Mountain: "Forget about throat and tongue, give up mouth and lips—now, how will you reveal it all, how say Way realized?"

"Why don't *you* forget and give up, old man?" countered Five-Peak.

"In a place without any people," said Hundred-Elder, "I've chopped my forehead wide open, and it's gazing straight at you!"

GATHA

Why don't you forget and give up, old man? Look,
look at all the sharp-tongued chatter in this dragon-and-snake battle!

It makes you think of that silent general whose arrows never missed,
or a lone osprey soaring ten thousand miles to the very edge of sky.

72

Hundred-Elder Throat Tongue

Hundred-Elder Mountain asked Cloud-Crag Mountain: "Forget about throat and tongue, give up mouth and lips—now, how will you reveal it all, how say Way realized?"

"Still clinging to them, old man?" replied Cloud-Crag.

"I'll never have dharma descendants now," lamented Hundred-Elder.

GATHA

Still clinging to them, old man? A sage Buddha-
lion with golden fur never cowers in the dirt. We travel Ch'an's[71]

ancient path together. And all this beneath old Hundred-Elder's
Valiant-Vast Peak: it's a mere snap of the fingers, useless, empty.

73

Patriarch Sudden-Horse Way-Entire's *Four Existential Distinctions and Hundred Negations*

A monk asked Grand-Master Sudden-Horse Way-Entire: "I'm done with clever ideas like the four existential distinctions and hundred negations. Please, Master, just point directly at that *ch'i*-weave mind Bodhidharma brought from the West."

"I'm exhausted today," replied Master Sudden-Horse, "I can't explain it for you. Go ask Wisdom-Hoard."

The monk journeyed away to ask Wisdom-Hoard, and Wisdom-Hoard said: "Why didn't you ask the master?"

"He told me to come ask you."

"I have a terrible headache today. I can't explain it for you. Go ask Hundred-Elder Mountain."

So, the monk traveled to Hundred-Elder Mountain, and asked. Hundred-Elder said: "I've gotten to the point that I don't understand it at all."

Finally, the monk went back to Grand-Master Sudden-Horse and told him what had happened. Sudden-Horse said: "Wisdom-Hoard's head is bright and clear. Hundred-Elder's head is dark and mysterious."[72]

GATHA

Hoard bright and clear, Elder dark and mysterious:
patchrobe monks with eyes full of enlightenment can't fathom that.

Sudden-Horse's foals trample everyone in all beneath heaven dead.
Even Purport Dark-Enigma didn't steal in broad daylight like this.

Done with the four distinctions and hundred negations:
in all heavenly and peopled realms, it's yours alone to understand.

74

Ox-Gold Rice Pail

Every time the seclusion-fast[73] came, Master Ox-Gold carried a pail of cooked rice out in front of the Sangha Hall and did a dance. Roaring with glorious laughter, he called out: "Hey all you bodhisattva cubs, come eat!"

Commenting on this, Snow-Chute Mountain said: "He did things like that, but Ox-Gold was hardly an awakened mind."

A century later, a monk asked Reward-Perpetua Mountain: "What wordless *ch'i*-weave insight was at work when that ancient said *Hey all you bodhisattva cubs, come eat!*?"

"It seems exactly like joyful praise celebrating the seclusion-fast," replied Reward-Perpetua.[74]

GATHA

Glorious laughter roaring beneath all that white cloud adrift,
Ox-Gold brings a pail of rice in both hands, offers it to us all.

If you too are a cub of that sage Buddha-lion with golden fur,[75]
you gaze three thousand miles and beyond in utter reverence.

75

Night-Crow Unjust Blows

A monk from Master Samadhi-Still Land's sangha came to visit Night-Crow Mountain. Night-Crow asked: "The dharma Samadhi-Still teaches—is it anything like what we teach here?"

"There's no difference," replied the monk.

"If there's no difference, go! Turn yourself around and go back there," shouted Night-Crow. Then he struck the monk a fierce blow with his abbot-staff.

"There's a watchful eye at the tip of that staff," said the monk. "You shouldn't be so careless with your blows."

"That was just one blow," countered Night-Crow. And he struck the monk three more times.

At that, the monk started to leave.

"People have been struck unjust blows from the beginning," called out Night-Crow.

The monk turned and said: "Maybe. But I notice the abbot-staff of authority is in your hands."

"If you like, this old mountain monk will give it back to you."

The monk stepped forward and grabbed the abbot-staff, then struck Night-Crow three blows.

"Unjust blows!" cried out Night-Crow. "Unjust blows!"

"People are struck unjust blows," replied the monk.

"You're just another oaf dealing out careless blows."

The monk thereupon bowed reverently.

"Is that how Master Samadhi-Still leaves?" asked Night-Crow.

Roaring with glorious laughter, the monk walked out.

"Things just melt away like that," mused Night-Crow Mountain. "They just melt away."

GATHA

To invite was easy,
to send away hard:
those two frolicking at that edge where the loom-of-origins unfurls,

watch them carefully. Oceans vast and deep turn to dust in a flash.
A goddess's gossamer sleeve slowly wears that kalpa-stone away.[76]

Old Night-Crow, old Night-Crow Mountain,
how many can equal you
handing him that abbot-staff at origins, magisterial Absence itself?

76

Cinnabar-Cloud Mountain's
Have You Eaten Yet

Cinnabar-Cloud Mountain asked a monk: "Where have you just come from?"

"From down below the mountain," replied the monk.

"Have you eaten yet?"

"I have."

"Didn't the person who served you that food possess the Buddha-deep eye's clarity whole?" asked Cinnabar-Cloud.

The monk was dumbfounded, speechless.

A century later, Reward-Perpetua Mountain asked Prosper-Nurture Mountain: "Anyone serving a monk food must be blessed with insight, so how could they not possess the Buddha-deep eye's clarity whole?"

"To be empty in giving, to be empty in receiving: both are a kind of blindness," replied Prosper-Nurture.

"And to exhaust everything the loom-of-origins opens before your eyes, is that too blindness?" asked Reward-Perpetua.

"You think I've mastered that kind of blindness?" exclaimed Prosper-Nurture.

GATHA

To exhaust everything the loom-of-origins opens
before your eyes: that's pure clarity, not blindness.

Why hold a grazing ox's head to the grass? Twenty-eight and six[77]
patriarchs offering a great dharma-treasure: it's sheer catastrophe,

sheer and profound catastrophe.
And where can you go looking
here, these heavenly and human realms all flooded over together?

77

Cloud-Gate Gruel-Cake

A monk asked Cloud-Gate Mountain: "What is small-talk that surpasses Buddhas and transcends patriarchs?"

"Gruel-cake," replied Cloud-Gate.[78]

GATHA

Small-talk that surpasses: there's no end of Ch'an pilgrims asking
questions. It's a fault-line gaping wide open. Can't you see? Look!

Cloud-Gate stuffs it full of gruel-cake, and they're still not settled.
Even today: all beneath heaven reveres the fairy tales teachers tell.

78

Bodhisattvas Filed into Bathhouse

In ancient times there were sixteen wide-open bodhisattvas. They all filed into the bathhouse one day—and just as they touched the water, they were suddenly awakened. All you Ch'an masters of heart-sight clarity, how can we realize their understanding? It's said that to probe deep mystery brings radiant enlightenment whole, our dwelling as Buddhamasters. But that just means moving through the days freely, your eight senses penetrating all the way in.

GATHA

To see through this with perfect clarity, a patchrobe monk
needs one thing: stretch out for a nap. And in your dreams,

if those bodhisattvas talk of pervasive awakening whole,
meet them leaving their fragrant baths, spit in their faces.

79

Dice-Thrown Mountain's *Mighty Farts*

A monk asked Dice-Thrown Mountain: "Isn't every sound the sound of Buddha's voice?"

"It is," replied Dice-Thrown.

"Then why spare us the blast of your mighty farts?"

Dice-Thrown struck the monk a blow.

"Obscene talk and sweet talk: don't they both belong to the first and foremost inner-pattern Way?" continued the monk.

"They do," replied Dice-Thrown.

"So I can use a mule's name for you? *Hee-haw! Hee-haw!*"

Dice-Thrown struck the monk another blow.

GATHA

Dice-Thrown! Dice-Thrown Mountain
free amid the wheeling loom-of-origins

seasons—giving one, getting two back,
becoming everything all here and there!

How wondrous: boundless people playing in Ch'an's risky surf
also finally tumble in deep and die. Then suddenly, waves alone

hiss and crash, hiss and crash
like a hundred rivers turned all topsy-turvy and cascading away.

80

Visitation-Land's *Tossed into Cascading Rapids*

A monk asked Visitation-Land: "Does a newborn child already have the six depths of consciousness?"[79]

"A little ball tossed into cascading rapids," replied Visitation-Land.

Later, the monk asked Dice-Thrown Mountain: "What wordless *ch'i-weave* insight is at work in *a little ball tossed into cascading rapids*?"

"One after another after another," mused Dice-Thrown, "thoughts flow on and on and never-ending on."

GATHA

Absence realized in our six depths of consciousness: it's the one question, where insight's always begun in our Ch'an household.

A little ball tossed into rapids cascading far and wide, on and on and never-ending on: who's free enough to watch it tumble away?

81

Medicine Mountain's
Monarch among Monarchs

A monk asked Medicine Mountain: "In a level field of low grass, monarch deer gather into a herd. How do you shoot the monarch among monarchs?"

"Watch out for that arrow!" cried Medicine.

The monk tumbled upside-down onto the ground.

"Attendant!" called out Medicine. "Drag this dead oaf out of here!"

The monk stood up and walked away.

"Playing games with mudballs," exclaimed Medicine Mountain, "doesn't that oaf know any limits?"

> Commenting on this, Snow-Chute Mountain said: "Three steps and you may live. Five steps and you surely die."

GATHA

Monarch among monarchs:
Watch! Watch very closely!

Medicine shot his one arrow,
the monk walked three steps:

still alive after five steps, you can yourself
gather monarch herds and chase tigers away.

It's always been clear-eyed hunters who perfect their aim. And so,
at the top of his lungs, Snow-Chute cries: *Watch out for that arrow!*

82

Vast-Dragon's *Strong and Enduring Dharma-Self*

A monk asked Vast-Dragon: "This self and the beautiful things of this world: they crumble into ruins. What is the strong and enduring dharma-self?"

"Mountain flowers opening like brocade," replied Dragon, "stream-water deep and clear as indigo-jade."

GATHA

Asking reveals what you don't know,
answering what you don't understand.

Among icy moonlight and high winds,
among ancient cliffs and cold junipers,

laugh remembering
you meet a sage-master of Way on the road,
meet him not with words and not with silence.

Take a jade sword to the black dragon's lair
and shatter the Buddha-truth pearl it guards:[80]

unless you shatter it clean
its flaws only grow worse.

In a nation full of rules and regulations,
there are three thousand ways to falter.

83

Cloud-Gate's *Wandered Pillars* in the Star River

Instructing the assembled sangha, Cloud-Gate Mountain said: "Ancient Buddhas wandered among those pillars topped with bowls gathering dew in the Star River:[81] how deep into the loom-of-origins is that?"

Answering for the sangha, he said: "On South Mountain, clouds rise. On North Mountain, rain falls."

GATHA

In South Mountain clouds
and North Mountain rains:
that's where you meet twenty-eight and six patriarchs face-to-face.[82]

How pervasive that enlightenment is: the Chinese drumbeat starts,
and already monks crowd Korean meditation halls, ready to dance.

Look for joy in sorrow,
and find sorrow in joy?
Who would say pure gold is the same as shit heaped on the ground?

84

Vimalakirti Dharma-Gate Nonduality

Vimalakirti asked Sutra-Kill Manjusri, regal teacher of Buddhas:[83] "How does a bodhisattva pass through the dharma-gate of nonduality?"[84]

"Here's my guess about these dharma-realm expanses,"[85] replied Manjusri. "No words and nothing said. No teaching and nothing learned. Free of questions and free of answers. That's how you pass through the dharma-gate of nonduality."

Then Manjusri asked Vimalakirti: "But we each say it in our own way. How would you say it? How does a bodhisattva pass through the dharma-gate of nonduality?"

> Commenting on this, Snow-Chute Mountain said: "What could old Vimalakirti say?"

> Commenting further, Snow-Chute Mountain said: "Broke it open!"

GATHA

AI-OO!—old Vimalakirti suffers such
empty sympathy for things, such grief,

lying sick in the hills of far-off India,
his thin body withered skin and bone.

Regal teacher of Buddhas, Manjusri
visits that room kept carefully swept,

and sage Vimalakirti turns on himself,
asking about some gate of nonduality.

Why turn on yourself?
Who ever finds absolute answers or that Buddha-lion with golden fur?[86]

85

Shrine-Hut Master Roars

A monk went to visit a shrine-hut master high on Kindred-Tree Mountain and asked: "If you meet a huge tiger up here, what will you do?"

The shrine-hut master roared a tiger's roar. The monk acted like he was terrified. The shrine-hut master laughed gloriously.

"You old thief!" shouted the monk.

"Why haggle with an old monk?" wondered the shrine-hut master. The monk gave up and left.

> Commenting on this, Snow-Chute Mountain said: "Here we have two
> malignant thieves, happy to just cover their ears and steal the bell."

GATHA

A tiger's quick. If you don't strike fast,
it's a thousand miles away, a mere idea:

gorgeous with elegant stripes rippling,
but no ferocity of claw and fang bared.

Haven't you seen
how those two wild tigers tangled beneath Valiant-Vast Mountain,[87]
shouts and axe-flashes scattering everywhere, the earth shuddering?

For a great sage-elder, seeing is Absence, is itself
seizing that tiger's tail—O—tiger's tail, and plucking its whiskers!

86

Cloud-Gate's *Kitchen. Granary. Three Gates.*

Teaching the assembled sangha, Cloud-Gate Mountain said: "Radiant enlightenment abides within each and every one of you. Those who look without seeing are dark within shadowy dark. How do you reveal this radiant enlightenment that everyone possesses?"

Answering for the sangha, he said: "Kitchen. Granary. Three gates."

He paused, and then continued: "Our grand and wondrous affairs can't compare with the Absence of simply doing nothing."

GATHA

Each alone in enlightenment, self-illuminated:
Cloud-Gate strings you together on one thread.

Once blossoms scatter, a tree casts no shadow.
Then, who among you looks without seeing it?

Seeing without seeing, you
ride that ox topsy-turvy—O—topsy-turvy into the Buddha Hall.[88]

87

Cloud-Gate Medicine Disease

Instructing the assembled sangha, Cloud-Gate Mountain said: "Medicine
and disease cure each other. The whole vast expanse of this world: it's all
medicine. And what are you yourself?"

GATHA

The whole expanse of this vast world: it's all medicine.
Ancients, moderns: how could they be so utterly wrong?

Just close your gate and forget about carts and carriages:
life's Buddha-road ahead is your own boundless silence.

Wrong! Utterly wrong!
That ox-herd rope leading the nose of your original-face: it's distant skies.[89]

88

Dark-Enigma-Sands Mountain's
Three Types of Invalid

Instructing the assembled sangha, Dark-Enigma-Sands said: "Old masters everywhere, they always talk about guiding people and enriching lives. But if I encounter the three types of invalid, how can I guide their lives? If I raise the mallet[90] to announce meditation practice or the Buddha-whisk to announce a dharma-talk, the blind one sees nothing. If I talk about three-shadowed-earth *samadhi*, the deaf one hears nothing. If I ask for explanation, the mute one says nothing. So how can I guide their lives? And if I can't guide them, what good is the Buddha-dharma?"

Later, a monk asked Cloud-Gate Mountain about this, and Cloud-Gate said: "Offer your bows."

The monk bowed reverently and rose. Cloud-Gate thrust at him with his travel-staff, and the monk jumped back. Cloud-Gate said: "You're clearly not blind."

Then he called the monk closer. When the monk approached, Cloud-Gate whispered: "You're clearly not deaf."

Finally, Cloud-Gate asked: "Do you understand?"

"I do not."

"And you're clearly not mute."

At this, the monk saw through things whole.

GATHA

Blind, deaf, perfectly mute: such dark
distances open in that loom-of-origins.

Heaven above, earth below: the whole
thing's a bundle of laughs and laments.

Eagle-eye master unable to see the sheer actuality of things,
perfect-pitch musician unable to hear a *ch'in*'s dark-enigma:[91]

why bother? How could it compare to sitting alone at an empty window?
Leaves falling and blossoms opening: things each have their own season.

> *Commenting further, Snow-Chute Mountain said:"Do you understand, or
> not? Iron hammer-head with no hole."*[92]

89

Cloud-Crag's *My Body Is Through-and-Through Hands and Eyes*

When they were monks together, Cloud-Crag Mountain asked Way-I Mountain: "What does that Bodhisattva of Great Compassion do with all those hands and eyes?"

"It's like someone in the night groping behind them for a pillow," replied Way-I.

"I understand."

"How would you reveal your understanding?" asked Way-I.

"My body is everywhere altogether hands and eyes."

"How utterly marvelous!" exclaimed Way-I. "You've captured Way perfectly! But that's only eighty percent."

"And how would you reveal it?" asked Cloud-Crag

"My body is through-and-through hands and eyes."

GATHA

My body is everywhere altogether,
my body is through and through—
even offered in open hands like this, insight's ten million miles away.

Two-Moon spreads its vast wings and soars through the six directions,[93]
wingbeats whirling up gale-storms that churn the four boundless seas:

what kind of dust storm is this—O—this world of dust suddenly wild,
and not the least—O—not the least hair's-breadth of things holds still?

Haven't you seen
how Indra's jewel-net cascades down, reflections seething reflections?[94]
Hands and eyes at the abbot-staff's tip—where could they come from?

AI-OO!

90

Wisdom-Gate *Prajna*-Awakening

A monk asked Wisdom-Gate Mountain: "What is the original potency of *prajna*-awakening?"

"Oyster holding a radiant moon in its mouth," replied Gate.

"And what is the actualization of *prajna*-awakening?" asked the monk.[95]

"Rabbit pregnant and full-bellied."

GATHA

In even one flake of empty stillness—words end, landscape felt
within ends. It's where the whole world can see emptiness born.

But oyster moon and dark-enigma rabbit: given such bottomless
insight, our Ch'an household just started bickering and fighting.

91

Salt-Legal Mountain Rhinoxeros

One day, Salt-Legal Mountain called out to the attending monk: "Bring me the fan with a rhinoxeros[96] painted on it."

"That fan's broken," answered the attending monk.

"If the fan's broken, bring me the rhinoxeros," demanded Salt.

The attending monk had no response.

Half a century later, answering for the monk, Dice-Thrown Mountain said: "I don't mind bringing it. But what if the horn isn't completely right?"

> Commenting on this, Snow-Chute Mountain said: "I want it wrong."

And also answering for the monk, Stone-Frost Mountain said: "If I returned it to you, Master, it would be pure Absence."

> Commenting on this, Snow-Chute Mountain said: "But the rhinoxeros would still be there."

A century later, Prosper-Sustain Mountain drew an origin-mind circle[97] in the dirt, and at its center wrote the ideogram *ox*, with its two horns.

> Commenting on this, Snow-Chute Mountain said: "Why didn't you bring it in the first place?"

And Prosper-Nurture Mountain called out: "He'd reached a venerable age, Master. Wasn't it time he stopped expecting perfection from people?"

> Commenting on this, Snow-Chute Mountain said: "Ah well. All that work for nothing."[98]

GATHA

That fan with a rhin*ox*eros painted on it: we use it all the time,
and people keep asking about it, but no one's ever had a clue.

Crystalline wind blowing boundless away, that horn's exactly
like clouds-and-rain love-making—once gone, gone for good.[99]

92

World-Honored-One Ascended

One day, the World-Honored-One[100] ascended to the teaching platform and sat. Sutra-Kill Manjusri, regal teacher of Buddhas,[101] sounded the announcement mallet and called out: "Behold the Dharma Emperor's dharma! Look closely! The Dharma Emperor's dharma is exactly this here before you!"

The World-Honored-One thereupon rose and descended from the teaching platform.

GATHA

In the crowd of sage-masters, maybe some monk understood
that Dharma Emperor's dharma-teaching isn't like this at all.

But if people there were in perfect accord with that teaching,
why would Manjusri swing his mallet to announce anything?

93

Lumen-Vast Little Dance

A monk asked Lumen-Vast Mountain: "What wordless *ch'i*-weave insight was at work when Reward-Perpetua Mountain spoke of *joyful praise cele-brating the seclusion-fast?*[102]

Lumen-Vast did a little dance. The monk bowed reverently.

"What did you just see that made you bow reverently like that?" asked Lumen-Vast.

The monk did a little dance.

"You're crafty as a wild-fox trickster-spirit!" exclaimed Lumen-Vast.[103]

GATHA

The first arrow broke through. And the second went deep, deep. Who calls yellow leaves pure gold? Sixth Patriarch's refuge Twofold-Creek

and the seething waves of that human realm: if there's no difference, these boundless lands will flood over, and people everywhere drown.

94

Hewn-Beam Not Seeing

The *Hewn-Beam Sutra* says: *When I'm not seeing original-nature,*[104] *why don't you look at the place I am when I'm not seeing original-nature? If you see that terrain clearly, you'll see occurrence-appearing-of-itself is nothing other than the very form of that not-seeing. If you don't see clearly, occurrence-appearing-of-itself seems to be something else. But how could it not be you yourself?*

GATHA

Elephant and ox: in the darkness of cataracts, they look the same.
And so, sage-monks have always seen patterns and named things.

But if you want to see old yellow-face Buddha today, wandering[105]
through monasteries and markets will only get you halfway there.

95

Reward-Perpetua Mountain's
Taught Two Different Ways

One day, Reward-Perpetua Mountain said: "You can say Buddha Existence-Tissue Arrival's[106] liberated Arhats were still tangled in the three poisons, but not that he taught two different ways, one for beginning students and one for advanced. I'm not saying he didn't teach, only that he didn't teach two different ways."

"How would you reveal Buddha Existence-Tissue Arrival's teaching?" Prosper-Nurture Mountain asked his friend.

"No deaf person could hear it," replied Reward-Perpetua.

"I can see you've been listening to that talk for beginners."

"So how would you reveal it?" asked Reward-Perpetua.

"I'd go sip some tea."

GATHA

Talk—O—there's talk for students advanced and beginning,
but isn't a sleeping dragon mirrored in water still and deep?

In Absence, you find clear water full of moonlight swelling;
and in Presence, waves rising without wind. Ch'an pilgrim

Reward-Perpetua became a dragon in Three-Cascade Gorge;[107]
and Prosper-Nurture's painted a beauty-spot bright onto his forehead.

96

Visitation-Land's *Three Hinge-Phrases*

To instruct the assembled sangha, Visitation-Land used three hinge-phrases:[108]

GATHA

1

A clay Buddha can't cross-over *through riverwater.*[109]
Second-Patriarch Radiance lit all heaven and earth?[110]

Standing one-armed in snow, steely and determined:
who wouldn't call it some strange kind of delusion?

2

A gold Buddha can't cross-over *through furnace heat.*
At Mongrol Purple-Calm's, monks passed a signboard

saying: *I have a fierce dog. Hesitate, and you're dead.*
But is there anywhere crystalline wind will not reach?

3

A wood Buddha can't cross-over *through blazing fire.*
I often think of Oven-Smasher: villagers worshipped

their oven, but smashing it with his staff, he suddenly
liberated its god, who set out perfectly free of himself.[111]

97

Diamond Sutra Worthless Bonehead

The *Diamond Sutra* says: *If someone derides you as a worthless bonehead, it's because the sins they committed in a previous life pitched them into evil ways. Once you realize this, you're free.*

GATHA

To seize the Buddha-truth pearl, you[112]
must master wild adoration's depths.[113]

Of all sage-masters foreign or native,
not one's transmitted Absence whole:

if anyone could, that destroyer Lord
Mara would be lost. O, Wary-Cloud,[114]

Wary-Cloud Buddhas, to fathom me[115]
you must be Absence whole yourself.

*Commenting further, Snow-Chute
Mountain said: "Broke it open!"*

98

West-Temple Two Wrongs

When Master Sky-Common Mountain was a pilgrim-monk wandering among teachers, he stopped to visit West-Temple Mountain. He kept repeating: "How could I say that I understand Buddha-dharma? I've looked and looked, and never found anyone who can explain it."

One day, seeing Sky-Common in the distance, West-Temple called out to him: "Hey, Sky-Common Ripple-Ease!"

Sky-Common looked up at West-Temple, who immediately shouted: "Wrong!"

Sky-Common started walking toward West-Temple, and West-Temple again shouted: "Wrong!"

Sky-Common continued, and when he reached West-Temple, West-Temple whispered: "Those two wrongs just now: were they my wrongs or your wrongs?"

"My wrongs."

"Wrong!" cried West-Temple.

A resigned Sky-Common started to leave. West-Temple called after him: "Why don't you stay for the summer session? We'll talk through those two wrongs." Sky-Common didn't pause: he set out walking.

Later, when he was himself an abbot, Sky-Common Mountain said to the assembled sangha: "Early in my years of pilgrimage, karmic winds carried me to West-Temple Mountain's monastery. I was wrong there, twice, and that Illumine-Thought elder wanted me to stay for the summer session. He thought we could talk through those wrongs. But I wasn't wrong—and I understood, even then as I set out for the south, why he *said* I was wrong."

GATHA

Ch'an people everywhere
adore their frivolous trivia:
they glut themselves on learning and wisdom, never making it

real. It's so laughably sad: old Sky-Common conjuring stories
about renouncing West-Temple and resuming his pilgrimage.

Wrong! Wrong!
West-Temple's crystalline wind dissolved him away in a flash.

> *Commenting further, Snow-Chute Mountain said: "Some
> patchrobe monk suddenly appears crying* Wrong! *Then,
> right here, there's Snow-Chute's* Wrong! *And are they any
> different than Sky-Common Mountain's two wrongs?"*

99

Nation-Teacher Prajna-Devotion's
Ten-Self Buddha

Emperor Source-Ancestral Awe asked Nation-Teacher[116] Prajna-Devotion: "What is the Ten-Self Buddha?"

"You are, at this very moment, tramping all over that Dharma-Nature Buddha's head," replied Prajna-Devotion.

"I don't understand."

"Give up this dream of mastering some dharma-nature all clarity crystalline pure."

GATHA

Teacher to the nation: such a powerful and commanding title,
and only the great Prajna-Devotion could inspire such renown:

counseling a true emperor at the great T'ang Dynasty's height,
teaching him how to trample all over Ten-Self Buddha's head,

and wielding that iron hammer, he shattered Buddha's golden
bones to pieces. So what is our all-beneath-heaven realm then?

And sunk deep in this three-thousand-ocean Cosmos of night,
who can raid black dragon's lair, seize the Buddha-truth pearl?[117]

100

Open-Hand Ridge's
Sword That Slices Drifting Feathers

A monk asked Open-Hand Ridge: "What is insight sharp as a sword that slices drifting feathers in two?"

"Each branch of coral raises up another moon," replied Open-Hand.

GATHA

Wanting to make the peaceless peaceful,
wanting to make the brilliant simpletons,

sometimes pointing, sometimes striking,
or trusting snow ignited with blazing sky,

great metalsmiths cannot—O—cannot sharpen this sword any further,
and they cannot—O—cannot polish it into some pure and final clarity.

How wondrous! How
boundlessly wondrous: every branch of coral raises up another moon!

Notes

Names work very differently in ancient China. We almost never think about the meaning of names, but in ancient China, it was all about meaning. Artist-intellectuals adopted names for their meanings, choosing meanings that they felt somehow expressed their essential artistic or philosophical natures. Ch'an monks and teachers followed this rule in especially dramatic ways, giving themselves "dharma-names" or adopting names of local mountains (which were themselves given meaningful names). As translation of ancient Chinese texts involves most fundamentally translating a culture, it follows that those names should be rendered not simply in their romanized form but according to their meanings: the Sixth Patriarch's name, *Hui Neng*, therefore becomes *Prajna-Able*, for example, and *Yün Men* becomes *Cloud-Gate Mountain*.

Chapter titles are divided between two forms: some use quotations from the sangha-case ("Open-Hand Ridge's *Source-Ancestral Teaching*," for example), and some are four-word set-phrases ("Bodhidharma Vast-Expanse Absence," for example). A set-phrase is a telegraphic four-word phrase that refers somehow to an ancient text or legend, distilling into four scarcely grammatical words all the dimensions of a story or anecdote or idea. The Chinese often use such set-phrases in writing and speech to make a complex point in an elegant and terse way, and there are so many set-phrases that they are collected in special dictionaries. In the two classic sangha-case collections to follow, titles are exclusively in this set-phrase form.

-----

1. Awake-Entire's commentary only survives because a century and a half later (ca. 1300), an imprecise version was reconstructed from fragmentary manuscripts that had survived.
2. That framework is entirely absent in earlier English translations of *The Blue-Cliff Record*, and indeed all Ch'an texts, because translators were unaware of these concepts. For more on the broad failure of existing Ch'an translations, see my

China Root, especially the Appendix: "Lost in Translation." There is also a general discussion in my *The Way of Ch'an,* Introduction (pp. 4ff.), and considerations of specific texts in a number of chapter Introductions.

3. For a full discussion of Ch'an meditation, see the two Meditation chapters in *China Root,* pp. 27–34 and 103–12.

4. For a full explanation of how sangha-cases functioned in Ch'an practice, see the Sangha-Case chapter in my *China Root* (pp. 113–19).

5. War-True was a very pious Buddhist in the conventional sense of sutra study and gaining merit through donations to Buddhist institutions.

6. **Absence:** see Key Terms, p. 214.

7. The first two lines of "Fact-Mind Inscription," for which see my *The Way of Ch'an,* p. 140.

8. **primal sage-emperor:** China's mythic history begins with a series of almost godlike emperors who created the landscape of China, humans, and the foundational elements of human civilization: fire, language, agriculture, government, etc.

9. **black dragon . . . Buddha-truth pearl:** For the dragon, see Key Terms, p. 218. In Ch'an storytelling, this black dragon coils around the Buddha-truth pearl, and heroically raiding the dragon's lair and seizing that pearl is goal of Buddhist practice, tantamount to enlightenment. This dragon clutching the pearl in its claws is the subject of many powerful paintings.

10. **Buddha-whisk:** Small whisk wielded as a symbol of authority by an abbot.

11. **Sixth Patriarch . . . dust:** From the seminal tale in *The Platform Sutra of the Sixth Patriarch* (see my *The Way of Ch'an,* p. 165ff.), where the Sixth Patriarch demonstrates his enlightenment in this poem:

> Original source-tissue *Bodhi*-awakening
> isn't a tree. Nowhere stands the brilliant
>
> mirror. Buddha-nature perennially such
> pure clarity—where could dust gather?

12. **sunyata:** see Glossary of Buddhist Terms p. 229.

13. **Three-Cascade Gorge:** Formed when the mythic Emperor Cobra sliced a passage for the Yellow River through mountains. Ascending the waters cascading through this gorge is a Ch'an metaphor for the practice leading to enlightenment, and that enlightenment is likened to a fish struck by lightning and transformed into a dragon that soars away through the sky. See also the *gathas* of Cases 60 and 95.

14. **eyelids pinched closed:** enlightenment is sometimes described as eyelids peeled away, leaving awakened sight wide open.

15. **gateway:** The term gateway (關) refers first to gateways in mountain passes at the frontier, which can be either locked to block passage or opened to allow passage. And so, the idea is that it is a gateway one must open and pass through into realization. As such, it figures prominently throughout the Ch'an

tradition, most notably in the third of the classic sangha-case collections: *No-Gate Gateway*.

Prosper-Nurture Mountain ... Reward-Perpetua Mountain ... Cloud-Gate Mountain: Dharma brothers of Kingfisher-Cliff Mountain and all historically important teachers who reappear in *The Blue-Cliff Record* and are probably commenting when they heard this story at their own far-flung monasteries.

16. **Patriarch Flood-Deva Risen:** Kanadeva, fifteenth in the legendary lineage of twenty-eight Indian patriarchs that preceded Bodhidharma, and known for his verbosity and argumentativeness.

17. **ninety-six ancient schools ... crimson banners of victory:** when these schools of philosophy in ancient India debated, the winner hoisted crimson banners to celebrate victory.

18. **black dragon:** see note 9.

19. Of all those disciples, only Mahakasyapa understood when Buddha held up the flower on Vulture Peak (see Key Terms, p. 225).

20. **thirty-three patriarchs:** the legendary lineage of twenty-eight Indian and six Chinese patriarchs that connect Ch'an directly to Buddha (Bodhidarma is both the twenty-eighth Indian and the first Chinese, hence thirty-three).

entered the tiger cave: The tiger, with its wild energy and fierce immediacy, is a figure for the Ch'an master. So, to enter the tiger cave is to brave the ferocity of a Ch'an master's wisdom and make it your own.

21. **ch'i:** see Key Terms, p. 217.

22. **Sitting long in meditation:** According to legend, Bodhidharma reached full enlightenment by sitting in "wall-gaze" meditation for nine years.

23. **travel-staff:** Rough-hewn walking-stick, perhaps seven feet tall, which is cut in the mountains and left mostly in its natural state. Carried by monks as they traveled the country visiting Ch'an monasteries to learn from different masters, the travel-staff came to symbolize essential Ch'an insight, original Buddha-nature, etc.

24. **black dragon ... Buddha-truth pearl:** see note 9.

25. **seed-time breath-space ... home:** 宇宙, which is generally translated "space and time." But that imposes a whole Western metaphysical scheme on the Chinese worldview. In fact, both ideograms contain the image for a roof at the top. Below that, 宇 has the image for breath spreading in the space beneath the roof, hence: "breath-space home," and 宙 has the image for a seed sprouting beneath the roof, hence: "seed-time home." All of this makes sense, of course, in the Taoist/Ch'an framework wherein reality is seen as a nurturing home and an organic and ever-emergent process of transformation.

26. **blind-turtle adepts:** In several sutras, the blind turtle represents people struggling in darkness to see the light of awakening.

27. **Shadowed-Emergence:** The everyday meaning of 微 is "faint/sparse/hidden," but in poetic and philosophic contexts it takes on cosmological/ontological dimensions: forms, the ten thousand things, just on the not-yet-emergent side of

the origin-moment—just as they are about to emerge from the formless ground of Absence, or just after they vanish back into that ground.

28. **Thatch-Hut Mountain:** Ch'an originated at East-Forest Monastery on Thatch-Hut Mountain in the third–fourth centuries C.E. (see my *The Way of Ch'an*, pp. 75ff.). Thatch-Hut has been a central presence in Ch'an and broader Chinese culture ever since, with many important figures visiting the mountain and its numerous monasteries in order to practice Ch'an, consult teachers, hike, write landscape poems, paint landscape paintings, etc.

29. **lotus blossom:** Because its exquisite beauty is rooted in mud and murky water, the lotus flower in conventional Buddhism is the image of pure Buddha-mind untainted by the world of compromise and struggle in which we live our everyday lives.

30. **South Mountain:** calling up such passages as "like the timelessness of South Mountain" in the ancient *Book of Songs*, poets often called local mountains "South Mountain" to suggest a kind of mythic stature as an embodiment of the elemental and timeless nature of the earth.

31. **travel-staff:** See note 23. Compare the way Cloud-Gate wields his travel-staff in Case 60.

32. **slicing eyelids away:** see note 14.

33. **seclusion-fast:** periods of seclusion during which monks intensified practice and ate especially simple meals.

34. **Sudden-Horse:** Patriarch Sudden-Horse Way-Entire (Ma Tsu), who was the teacher of Hundred-Elder Mountain (Pai Chang).

35. **gate:** Recurring often in *The Blue-Cliff Record* and throughout the Ch'an tradition, *gate* refers to the courtyard gate through which one enters a monastery (or any traditional Chinese dwelling). Its complementary and more explicitly philosophical meaning is "an entrance-way to insight." And so, to pass through the gate is to attain enlightenment.

36. **potency:** see Key Terms, p. 218.

37. **original-face:** our inherently enlightened original-nature, also described as Buddha-mind or empty-mind.

38. **kalpa:** a world-cycle of 4,300,000 years.

39. Wellspring-South was Visitation-Land's teacher for decades, and the teacher under whom he attained enlightenment.

40. **original-face:** see note 37.

41. *samadhi*: see Glossary of Buddhist Terms, p. 229.

42. **Yellow-Bitterroot:** Purport Dark-Enigma's teacher, Yellow-Bitterroot Mountain. See Index of Ch'an Figures, p. 231.

43. **origin-mind circle:** Widely known by its later Japanese name, *enzo,* an origin-mind circle is the image of emptiness drawn with *wu-wei* spontaneity. Hence, it is a distillation of enlightenment's most basic and essential nature.

44. **Buddha-truth pearl:** See note 9. Here it seems the figure of a pearl is superimposed on the form of an origin-mind circle.

45. **Cold Mountain:** Legendary Ch'an poet who lived near a monastery on Cold

Mountain and ridiculed the monks who so earnestly practiced without realizing they were already enlightened. See my *The Way of Ch'an*, p. 187ff.

46. **Manjusri:** A mythological bodhisattva described as teacher to the Seven Buddhas of mythic antiquity who lived in successive kalpas (world-cycles each lasting 4,300,000 years), one per kalpa, the last of which was Shakyamuni Buddha. Manjusri is also described as embodying the wisdom of all Buddhas. In Sanskrit, Manjusri means "Gentle Glory," but as one might expect in Ch'an, the Chinese transliteration (文殊) means something like "Sutra-Kill."

   This encounter comes from a legend in which Absence-Belong made a pilgrimage to Lucid-Chill Mountain, where Manjusri conjured a monastery and hosted Absence-Belong. As he was leaving, Absence-Belong looked back and saw that the monastery had vanished, leaving only mountains.

47. **Swirl-Roam:** A reference to Old Swirl-Roam (盤古: P'an Ku), who was a primordial human-like creature who evolved from primal chaos. When he died, his body became the Cosmos.

48. **three realms:** In conventional Buddhism, this is traditionally given as: desire, form, and formlessness. In Ch'an, it would mean something like Absence, Presence, and the generative force driving the process of change, as Absence generates the ten thousand things of Presence in perpetual transformation.

49. *samsara*: see Glossary of Buddhist Terms, p. 229.

50. **Absence no-dharma:** This is another example of the philosophically productive double meaning of 無 ("no/Absence"). For 無法 can mean either "Absence-dharma" or "no dharma." Hence, the translation here combines the two possibilities: "Throughout the three realms of our everyday *samsara* universe, there is no dharma anywhere" and "Throughout its three realms, this everyday *samsara* universe is all Absence-dharma."

51. **ch'in:** Ancient stringed instrument much revered by Chinese intellectuals as a means for attaining enlightenment, the *ch'in* often appears in poems and was used as accompaniment when Chinese poets chanted their poems. In the hands of a master, a *ch'in* could voice with profound clarity the rivers-and-mountains realm, empty-mind, even the very source of all things.

52. **Buddha-lion with golden fur:** a recurring figure suggesting a number of references, all of which are perhaps in play and blurring together here: the lion ridden by Manjusri (see note 46), bodhisattva of wisdom; an earlier incarnation of Buddha; a sage with mature practice and penetrating insight.

53. **Sangha-Fundament:** Seng Chao (374–414), early scholar-monk who was instrumental in amalgamating Ch'an from native Taoism and imported Buddhism. See my *The Way of Ch'an*, pp. 78ff.

54. **potency:** see Key Terms, p. 218.

55. **rolled out three balls:** A story in the Ch'an record describes how Snow-Peak Mountain, seeing his student Dark-Enigma-Sands Mountain coming, rolled out three balls in front of him. Dark-Enigma-Sands pretended to smash the balls. Snow-Peak approved.

56. **dharma-nature:** the sheer thusness of things, which is the true teaching.

57. **six depths of consciousness:** the five senses, plus the awareness of consciousness.

58. *cross-beyond*: In conventional Buddhism, to "cross-beyond" means specifically to cross over into nirvana.

59. **Bodhidharma . . . sandal:** According to legend, Bodhidharma returned to India after he died. A traveler returning to China encountered him on the road carrying a sandal. When the traveler reached China, he reported his sighting to the emperor, who ordered that Bodhidharma's tomb be opened. Nothing was found in the tomb but a single sandal.

60. See Case 2 for this teaching by Visitation-Land.

61. Again (like Case 57) and more extensively repeating the beginning of Case 2.

62. **travel-staff:** see note 23.

63. Compare how Cloud-Gate wields his travel-staff in Case 22.

64. **Three-Cascade Gorge:** see note 13.

65. **seed-time breath-space home:** see note 25.

66. **Peace-Perpetua:** Ch'ang-an, the capital of China.
    idleness: see Key Terms, p. 221.

67. Referencing Sixth Patriarch Prajna-Able's enlightenment poem (see my *The Way of Ch'an*, p. 167):

    > Mind is the *Bodhi*-awakening tree,
    > body where a brilliant mirror stands,
    >
    > original source-tissue mirror such
    > pure-clarity—what could dust stain?

68. **Yellow-Nest . . . sword:** Yellow-Nest had recently led a powerful rebellion against oppressive T'ang rulers, during which he conquered Peace-Perpetua, the capital. It is said the rebellion began when a sword fell from heaven for Yellow-Nest's use—a kind of divine sanction.

69. The story in Case 1 similarly describes pious Emperor War-True questioning Bodhidharma, and being shocked at the answer. Master Remembrance-Treasure also appears there. The *gatha* commentary that follows refers explicitly to that story, where Bodhidharma flees across the river and into the north.

70. **origin-mind circle:** see note 43.

71. **Buddha-lion with golden fur:** see note 52.

72. **Wisdom-Hoard . . . Hundred-Elder:** Dharma brothers who had received dharma transmission together from Patriarch Sudden-Horse Way-Entire.

73. **seclusion-fast:** see note 33.

74. See Case 93 for an elaboration on this response.

75. **Buddha-lion with golden fur:** see note 52.

76. **goddess . . . kalpa-stone:** This kalpa-stone is said to be forty miles across. A goddess brushes her gossamer sleeve over the stone every hundred years—and when the stone is eroded away, a kalpa has passed. This supposedly requires 4,300,000 years.

77. **Twenty-eight and six patriarchs:** the twenty-eight Indian and six Chinese patriarchs in the legendary lineage connecting Ch'an directly to Buddha.

78. For the original version of this encounter in Cloud-Gate Mountain's teaching record, see my *The Way of Ch'an*, p. 240.

79. **six depths of consciousness:** see note 57.

80. **black dragon . . . Buddha-truth pearl:** see note 9.

81. **Star River:** our Milky Way.

82. **Twenty-eight and six patriarchs:** see note 77.

83. **Vimalakirti:** The scene described here is the setting of the *Vimalakirti Sutra*. Vimalakirti suffers a sickness that comes from his deep sympathy for the suffering of this world, and indeed his name in Chinese means something like Touch-Allied. Sage Vimalakirti was known for his fundamental critique of Buddhist teachings by asserting radical nonduality: that there is no basis for the oppositions essential to Buddhist teaching: samsara and nirvana, delusion and awakening, etc.
    Manjusri: See note 46.

84. **nonduality:** Existence-tissue reality seen as an undifferentiated whole, with no difference between Absence and Presence, delusion and awakening, subjective and objective (and in the terminology of conventional Buddhism, *samsara* and nirvana). And because words and thoughts create these distinctions, it is empty-mind that makes this nondual perspective possible.

85. **dharma-realm expanses:** the physical universe in all its thusness.

86. **Buddha-lion with golden fur:** see note 52.

87. This refers to a story similar to that told in this sangha-case, involving Hundred-Elder Mountain and his student Yellow-Bitterroot Mountain. In that story, when Yellow-Bitterroot roars a tiger's roar, Hundred-Elder strikes fast: he grabs an axe and starts to swing at Yellow-Bitterroot, but Yellow-Bitterroot dodges in and lands a fierce blow. Hundred-Elder returned to his rooms laughing uproariously.

88. **ox:** Ch'an figure for everyday mind with its unbridled process of thought after thought—from the *Ox-Herding Tale*, for which see note 89 below.

89. **ox-herd rope leading:** The famous *Ten Ox-Herding Pictures* recounts the tale of an ox-herd taming an ox, which represents the mind with its wayward and unmanageable thoughts. In part this involves leading the ox with a rope attached to its nose. Each picture is accompanied by a poem—and dismantling the idea that Ch'an is a battle against the wandering thoughts natural to our minds, this line plays on a line from the second of those poems: "Distant skies: how can you hide an ox's nose there?"
    original-face: see note 37.

90. **mallet:** wooden mallet struck against a wooden board in monasteries to announce meditation practice or a dharma-talk.

91. *ch'in:* See note 51.

92. **Iron hammer-head with no hole:** Fitting a handle into such a hammer-head was a Ch'an figure for the challenge of attaining Ch'an insight. See Case 14.

93. **Two-Moon:** mythic bird from the opening sequence of the *Chuang Tzu*, which begins:

> In Northern Darkness there lives a fish called Bright-Posterity. This Bright-Posterity is so huge that it stretches who knows how many thousand miles. When it changes into a bird, it's called Two-Moon. This Two-Moon has a back spreading who knows how many thousand miles, and when it thunders up into flight, its wings are like clouds hung clear across the sky. It churns up the sea and sets out on its migration to Southern Darkness, which is the Lake of Heaven.

94. **Indra's jewel-net:** Indra is the god of sky and divine guardian of the dharma. Surrounding his palace is a boundless net of jewels, each of which reflects all the other jewels and also all the reflections in all those jewels. An image for the complete interpenetration of all things, especially the sangha of all sentient beings, and a profound vision of the Cosmos as a tissue of mutual interrelation, even mutual identity. This has recently been adopted by deep ecologists as an image for earth's interwoven ecosystem.

95. *potency . . . actualization:* see Key Terms, p. 218.

96. *Rhinoceros* is 犀牛: literally, *rhinoceros* + *ox*. Both ideograms contain the graph for ox: 牛, which is a pictograph of an ox-head with ears and two horns, clearly seen in this early oracle-bone graph: ⱴ. This becomes important as the sangha-case unfolds.

97. **origin-mind circle:** see note 43.

98. These characters lived centuries apart from one another—but interestingly, they are portrayed as contemporaries in this exchange.

99. **clouds-and-rain love-making:** From the legend of a prince who, while staying at Shamaness Mountain, was visited in his sleep by a beautiful woman who said that she was the goddess of Shamaness Mountain. She spent the night with him, and as she left said: "At dawn I marshal the morning clouds; at nightfall I summon the rain."

100. **The World-Honored-One:** Shakyamuni Buddha.

101. **Manjusri:** see note 46.

102. See Case 74 for the source of this quote, and Case 24 for "seclusion-fast."

103. **fox:** The fox was popularly seen as a crafty trickster-spirit that can wreak havoc in your life. And so it is an image for clever over-intellectualizing that is the opposite of direct Ch'an insight.

104. *seeing original-nature:* 見性, the term that means enlightenment in Ch'an, and that derives from Bodhidharma's seminal definition of enlightenment: "seeing original-nature, you become Buddha." See Key Terms, p. 225. See also my *China Root*, p. 127, and *The Way of Ch'an*, p. 123.

105. **yellow-face Buddha:** yellow is, in Chinese, the color of earth.

106. **Buddha Existence-Tissue Arrival:** see Key Terms, p. 216.

107. **dragon in Three-Cascade Gorge:** see note 13.

108. **hinge-phrase:** A hinge-phrase (轉語) is a surprising and revelatory comment uttered by either a master or a student. Uttered by a master, it opens a

profound realization in a student, an awakening. Uttered by a student, it reveals that the student has attained such a realization or awakening.

109. **cross-over:** in conventional Buddhism, to "cross-over" or "cross-beyond" into nirvana.

110. **Second-Patriarch Radiance:** The Second Patriarch's full name is Radiance Spirit-Lightning. The story of his enlightenment in the snow is told in Case 41 of the *No-Gate Gateway* sangha-case collection:

> Bodhidharma sat facing a wall. The Second Patriarch stood outside in the snow. To prove his determined sincerity, he cut off his arm and presented it to Bodhidharma, then said: "Your disciple's mind is not yet silent. Please, Master, silence this mind."
> "Bring your mind here," replied Bodhidharma, "and I'll silence it for you."
> "I've searched and searched, but I can't find my mind."
> "There, you see, I've silenced your mind through and through."

111. **Oven-Smasher . . . :** A village shrine had a sacred oven where people sacrificed many creatures. One day, unhappy about all those animals dying, an abbot went to that village and rapped on the oven with his staff. The oven thereupon broke into pieces and a god emerged who said he had been cursed by karmic retribution and thanked the abbot for liberating him. The abbot came to be known as Oven-Smasher.

112. **black dragon . . . Buddha-truth pearl:** see note 9.

113. **adoration:** A crucial concept from the beginnings of Ch'an in Hsieh Ling-yün, *adoration* (賞) denotes an aesthetic experience of the wild rivers-and-mountains realm "mirrored" in empty-mind as a single overwhelming whole. As such, it was for Hsieh the pathway to awakening, conceived as dwelling integral to Tao's grandest manifestation in rivers-and-mountains landscape. See also my *The Way of Ch'an*, p. 95.

114. **Mara:** A kind of demon or devil in traditional Buddhism, Mara was a powerful deity symbolizing the sensual realm of desire that prevents beings from achieving enlightened liberation from rebirth and thus conquering death. In myth, he tried to stop Buddha's quest for enlightenment by tempting him with sensual pleasures. In Ch'an, though, once you become Absence, your identity is nothing less than the entire process of transformation. In this, you are enlightened and deathless, for that process continues forever.

115. **Wary-Cloud:** meaning of the Chinese transliteration for the Sanskrit *Gautama*.

116. **Nation-Teacher:** Prajna-Devotion (Nan-Yang Hui-Chung) was appointed to this position by this emperor, who took him as his personal teacher.

117. **black dragon . . . Buddha-truth pearl:** see note 9.

Key Terms

AN OUTLINE OF CH'AN'S
CONCEPTUAL WORLD

CH'AN'S CONCEPTUAL WORLD is described fully in my *China Root: Taoism, Ch'an, and Original Zen*. That book serves as the full philosophical introduction to this one. But Ch'an's conceptual world is easily outlined by defining a few foundational terms/concepts that recur often in the Ch'an literature. In fact, these concepts are inevitably crucial when Ch'an touches philosophical ground; but they have been misconstrued, mistranslated, and often simply untranslated—a process that has largely erased original Ch'an from modern Zen.

Our understanding of Ch'an/Zen changes dramatically when we realize that these terms all come from early Taoist philosophy. By probing deeper into the native understanding of key terms/concepts, a new Ch'an is revealed. It is a Ch'an grounded in the rich earth of Taoist cosmology/ontology, reality experienced as a generative tissue—a Ch'an for which spiritual practice aspires to reintegrate consciousness with that tissue in perpetual transformation. Concepts at this foundational level blur, and Taoist terminology proliferates. So, what we find here in a survey of Ch'an's key terms is a host of concepts, often nearly synonymous, each offering a different way into the fundamental nature of consciousness and Cosmos.

This Key Terms section functions as a glossary to those terms/concepts, and it is also designed to be read straight through as a short essay introducing Ch'an's conceptual framework—which means, unfortunately, it cannot follow alphabetical order. Here is an alphabetical index to the terms:

PRESENCE 有

The empirical universe, described in Taoist philosophy as the ten thousand things in their perennial transformations.

ABSENCE 無

The generative source-tissue from which the ever-changing realm of Presence perpetually arises. This undifferentiated tissue is the ontological substrate infused mysteriously with a generative energy. We might almost describe it in scientific terms as matter itself: the formless material that is shaped into the ten thousand discrete forms of reality (Presence) and into which those forms dissolve at death. Because of its generative nature, it continuously shapes itself into the individual forms of the Cosmos, then reshapes itself into other forms: the ten thousand things in the constant process of change. So, a more literal translation of Absence might be "without form," in contrast to "within form" for Presence. Absence is known directly in meditation, where it is experienced as empty consciousness itself, known in Ch'an terminology as "empty-mind" or "no-mind" (see below): the formless generative source of both thoughts and the ten thousand things. Hence, meditation as a spiritual practice reintegrating consciousness and Cosmos.

WAY (TAO) 道

The Tao of Taoism. *Tao* originally meant "way," as in "pathway" or "roadway," a meaning it has kept. But Lao Tzu reconceived it as a generative cosmological process, an ontological "path*Way*" by which things come into existence, evolve through their lives, and then go out of existence, only to be transformed and reemerge in a new form. As such, it might provisionally be divided into Presence and Absence. Here is a prime example of overlapping terminology struggling to name the fundamental nature of reality, for in practice Way/Tao emphasizes the undifferentiated and generative nature of the existence-tissue, and is therefore nearly synonymous with Absence. Indeed, Lao Tzu describes it as "source" and "female" and "mother."

Tao represents one of the most dramatic indications that Ch'an is a refinement and extension of Taoism, because the term *Tao* is used extensively in Ch'an with the same meaning. It sometimes simply means "Ch'an's *way* of practice, its path*Way* to enlightenment," a usage that parallels its early use in Taoism and Confucianism. But more often, and more philosophically important, it is the Taoist Way/Tao, that generative ontological source-tissue. And sometimes it is both simultaneously, as in the quintessential Ch'an dictum: "Ordinary mind is Way."

DARK-ENIGMA 玄

Perhaps the most foundational concept in this Taoist-Ch'an cosmology/ ontology, *dark-enigma* is Way before it is named, before Absence and Presence give birth to one another—that region beyond name and ideation where consciousness and the empirical Cosmos share their source. *Dark-enigma* came to have a particular historic significance, for it became the name of a neo-Taoist school of philosophy in the third and fourth centuries C.E.: Dark-Enigma Learning (see my *The Way of Ch'an*, p. 47ff.), a school that gave Chinese thought a decidedly ontological turn and became central to the synthesis of Taoism and *dhyana* Buddhism into Ch'an. And indeed, the concept is at the very heart of Ch'an practice and enlightenment. It is there at the very beginning, concluding the first chapter of the *Tao Te Ching*: "dark-enigma deep within dark-enigma, / gateway of all mystery." And it recurs often at key moments throughout the Ch'an tradition. Among the countless examples is Fathom Mountain (Tung Shan) saying that the most profound dimension of Ch'an's wordless teaching is dark-enigma within dark-enigma, which he evocatively describes as the "tongue of a corpse." And the very influential Stone-Head (Shih T'ou) ends his still-influential poem "Amalgam-Alike Compact" declaring dark-enigma to be the essential object of Ch'an inquiry:

Please, you who try to fathom dark-enigma clear
through, don't pass your days and nights in vain.

EXISTENCE-TISSUE 如

如 is virtually synonymous with Absence, Tao, and dark-enigma: reality as a single tissue, undifferentiated and generative. The vast and ongoing transformation of things is this *existence-tissue* coalescing into individual forms and then dispersing back into a single undifferentiated tissue. And it is important for Ch'an that this tissue is the "thusness" we encounter every moment in our everyday life, as emphasized in the recurring phrase 真如: "existence-tissue all thusness-clarity absolute."

THUSNESS, ETC. 真

The sheer presence of reality in and of itself, free of our ideas and stories: reality experienced as sheer wonder and mystery. There is no end to Ch'an stories revealing this thusness as the whole of Ch'an, as the most profound of teachers, especially in its most magisterial form as rivers-and-mountains landscape. As such, it returns consciousness to empty-mind or mirror-mind (see p. 224), wherein its "clarity-absolute" becomes the very content of consciousness or identity: a major dimension of awakening.

CH'I 氣

氣 is often described as the universal life-force breathing through things. But this presumes a dualism that separates reality into matter and a breath-force (spirit) that infuses it with life. Like the Absence/Presence dichotomy, that dualism may be useful as an approach to understanding; but more fully understood, *ch'i* is both breath-force and matter simultaneously. It is a single tissue generative through and through, the matter and energy of the Cosmos seen together as a single breath-force surging through its perpetual transformations. And so, *ch'i* is nearly synonymous with Way and Absence, but emphasizing their generative dynamism.

INNER-PATTERN 理

The philosophical meaning of *inner-pattern*, which originally referred to the veins and markings in a precious piece of jade, is something akin to what we call natural law. It is the system of principles or patterns that governs the unfolding of *Way* (or Absence, or *ch'i*) into the various forms of the ten thousand things in their perennial transformations. It is a pervasive concept in the Ch'an tradition, where moving integral to inner-pattern is one definition of awakening.

POTENCY 體
ACTUALIZATION 用

Together, *potency* and *actualization* represent an important pair of foundational cosmological/ontological concepts in Chinese philosophy. *Potency* refers to the inherent potentiality or nature of things: a virtual synonym for *inner-pattern*. That "potency" gives shape to the particular "actualization," the ongoing emergence (expression/manifestation) of things in the world.

LOOM-OF-ORIGINS 機

A mythological description of Way's unfurling process. Hence, the Cosmos in its perennial transformation seen as an ever-generative loom-of-origins. Chuang Tzu, the seminal Taoist sage, describes it like this: "The ten thousand things all emerge from a loom-of-origins, and they all vanish back into it."

DRAGON 龍

Another mythical incarnation of Way and its ten thousand things tumbling through their traceless transformations, dragon was feared and revered as the awesome force of change, as the embodiment of all creation and all destruction. Its form was therefore in constant transformation. To take one example: small as a silkworm and vast as all heaven and earth, dragon descends into deep waters in autumn, where it hibernates until spring, when its reawakening means the return of life to earth. It rises and ascends into sky, where it billows into thunderclouds and falls as spring's life-bringing rains. Its claws flash as lightning in those thunderclouds, and its rippling scales glisten in the bark of rain-soaked pines.

HEAVEN AND EARTH 天地

Heaven has a number of intertwined meanings that often function simultaneously. Originally a kind of impersonal divinity, the seminal Taoist sages reinvented heaven as an entirely empirical phenomenon—the generative cosmological force that drives the ongoing transformation of natural process—thereby secularizing the sacred while at the same time investing the secular with sacred dimensions. This transition moment was soon superseded by the entirely secular *Way (Tao)*, which was essentially synonymous with *heaven*, but without the metaphysical implications.

Heaven appears often in the phrase "heaven and earth," meaning the world of our everyday experience, for 天 means most simply "sky." But the phrase also means "the universe" in Taoism's cosmological sense, for *heaven and earth* were conceived as the grandest cosmological manifestations of *yang* and *yin*. Hence, the universe conceived as a living and dynamic interpenetration of *yang* and *yin*.

From this comes a second set of terms for heaven and earth: 乾 and 坤. These terms, the titles of the first two hexagrams of the *I Ching*, emphasize heaven as *yang* (the active generative force of the Cosmos) and earth as *yin* (the receptive generative force): the two forces whose ceaseless interaction generates the process of change. Accordingly, 乾 and 坤 might be read as "creative" and "receptive."

OCCURRENCE-APPEARING-OF-ITSELF   自然

A central concept in early Taoist cosmology/ontology, 自然 *(tzu-jan)* is a way of describing the process of Way that emphasizes individual entities rather than the process as a whole. Its literal meaning is "self-so" or "the of-itself," which, as a philosophical concept, becomes "being such of itself," hence "spontaneous" or "natural." But a more revealing translation of *tzu-jan* is "occurrence-appearing-of-itself," for the term is meant to describe the ten thousand things burgeoning forth spontaneously from the generative source (Presence from Absence), each according to its own nature, independent and self-sufficient, each dying and returning to the process of change, only to reappear in another self-generating form. As such, this inheritance from Taoism continued as a major element in Ch'an's conceptual framework.

ABSENCE-ACTION   無為

If there is a single term that describes the nature of sangha-case practice (see Introduction p. ix) and Ch'an enlightenment, it is 無為

(*wu-wei*). Like *tzu-jan*, w*u-wei* dates to the earliest levels of Taoist thought, and means literally "no/Absence" (*wu*) + "acting" (*wei*). A spiritual practice broadly adopted by ancient artist-intellectuals, it became central to Ch'an practice—further indication of Ch'an's essentially Taoist nature. *Wu-wei* means "not acting" in the sense of acting without the metaphysics of self, or of being *absent* when you act. This selfless action is the movement of *tzu-jan*, so *wu-wei* means acting as an integral part of *tzu-jan's* spontaneous burgeoning forth out of Absence into Presence.

Wu-wei is perhaps the original exploitation of the double meaning of 無 (no/Absence) that became crucial in Ch'an. Examples include *unborn/Absence-born* and *no-mind/Absence-mind* (for which, see below), and a host of other variations: *no/Absence knowing, no/Absence thought, no/Absence form, no/Absence dwelling, no/Absence dharma, no/Absence practice, no/Absence enlightenment.* This double meaning opens to the deepest level of *wu-wei's* philosophical complex, where the term's alternate sense of "Absence" + "acting" means *wu-wei* action is action directly from, or indeed *as* the ontological source. We see in sangha-cases Ch'an masters dramatizing this in their wild antics (behavior that likens them to Chuang Tzu's zany Taoist sages): to practice *wu-wei* is to move with the wild energy of the Cosmos itself. But it also takes the form of unbridled mental processes: indeed, the *Lamp-Transmission Record* says "*wu-wei* is meditation." Taken altogether, *wu-wei* represents a return to Paleolithic consciousness. And it is, again, the very definition of Ch'an enlightenment, enlightenment that is ideally the form of everyday life.

SOURCE-ANCESTRAL   宗

In the blur of concepts at deep cosmological/ontological levels, *source-ancestral* seems virtually indistinguishable from Way or Absence or inner-attern, and it is at times described as equivalent to Absence-action (*wu-wei*). The full dimensions of this concept are revealed dramatically in the etymologies of its two pictographic elements: 宀 and 示. 宀 simply means "roof," and is a stylized version of 𠆢, the early form that portrays a side-view of the traditional Chinese roof with its prominent ridge-line and curved form. 示 derives from 川 and the more ancient oracle-bone form 示, showing heaven as the line above, with three streams of light emanating earthward from the three types of heavenly bodies: sun, moon, and stars. These three sources of light were considered bright distillations of, or embryonic origins of *ch'i*, the breath-force that pulses through the Cosmos as both matter and energy simultaneously. Hence, 宗 is the cosmological source of *ch'i* as a dwelling-place, a dwelling-place that is the very source of the Cosmos.

The common meaning of 示 was simply "altar," suggesting a spiritual space in which one can be in the presence of those celestial *ch'i*-sources. And indeed, enlightenment in Ch'an was to inhabit this dwelling-place altar, as it was for Chuang Tzu who described a sage as one who "holds fast to the source-ancestral." And indeed, the common meaning of 宗 is "ancestor," which suggests a remarkable sense of the source as ancestral to us, as kindred. And so, the source-ancestral as always already our very nature.

IDLENESS 閑, 閒

Way unfurls its process of transformation in an effortless and spontaneous movement that can be described as idleness. Recognizing this, ancient China's artist-intellectuals and Ch'an adepts took living in idleness as a spiritual ideal, a kind of meditative wandering in which you move with the improvisational movement of Absence-action. And so, it is Absence-action enacted in the context of everyday life.

Etymologically, the character for *idleness* connotes "profound serenity and quietness," its pictographic elements rendering a tree standing alone within the gates to a courtyard: 閑, combining two pictographic elements more clearly visible in their early forms as 門 (gate: showing double doors) and 木 (tree: showing a trunk with branches above and roots below). Or in its alternate form, a moon shining through open gates: 閒, which replaces 木 with 月 (moon).

UNBORN (ABSENCE-BORN) 無生

無生 plays on the two meanings of 無 in much the same way as 無為 (*wu-wei*), to give: "no/Absence (*wu*) + born/alive (*sheng*)." 無生 means "not living" in the sense of living with the metaphysics of self *absent*, hence: "selfless living." This opens to a deeper level in which the term means "Absence-born" or "Absence-alive," describing our most essential identity as Absence itself. And finally, 無生 also means "not born" or "unborn," describing the fact that we are each a fleeting form conjured in Tao's process of perpetual transformation: not just born out of it and returned to it in death, a familiar concept that still assumes a center of identity detached from the Cosmos and its processes, but never *out of it*, totally unborn. Indeed, our fullest identity, being unborn, is Way itself, and therefore all and none of earth's fleeting forms simultaneously. And so, the double meaning is beautifully complementary, for to be "unborn" is precisely to be "Absence-born/alive." This unborn dwelling is the goal of sangha-case practice.

EMPTINESS 空, 虛

In its native Taoist and Dark-Enigma Learning context, *emptiness* is essentially synonymous with *Absence*: emptiness in the sense of undifferentiated reality *empty* of individual forms, reality as a single formless and generative tissue to which we belong. It was used to (mis-)translate the Sanskrit *sunyata* (for which, see Glossary of Buddhist Terms, p. 229), a crucial moment in the creation of Ch'an. Free of the metaphysical dimensions of *sunyata*, 空 and 虛 are entirely this-worldly, notably in their common meaning "sky," archetypal form of emptiness in our everyday experience. Etymologically, the two elements of 空 portray *labor* (工, early form 舌—suggesting something emerging from an absence, and labor is of course to make something where there was nothing) within a *cave* (穴, indicating the space beneath a roof 宀, stylized version of ∩, side-view of the traditional Chinese roof with its prominent ridge-line). Hence, a generative emptiness in earth, a womb where the work of gestation happens. 虛 in its early forms contains a pair of mountain peaks (△) and, in the space above those peaks, the element for *tiger* (虍, deriving from early images like 虎). Together, these two elements form 虛, literally: "mountain tiger-sky." This emphasizes the sense of emptiness as sky/heaven: however, rather than emptiness as mere stillness (as in conventional Buddhism), it is emptiness dynamic with the wild energy of a tiger. And so, the two complementary terms (which often appear together in Ch'an texts) suggest at their origins something like emptiness in its heavenly and earthly forms, and *heaven and earth* is a Chinese term for the Cosmos itself.

MIND 心
CH'I-WEAVE MIND 意

In Ch'an parlance, *mind* principally refers to consciousness emptied of all contents, a state revealed through deep meditation: hence, mind as "original-nature" or "Buddha-nature." This consciousness in its original-nature is nothing other than Absence, that generative cosmological tissue—for it is the empty source of thought and memory, and also an empty mirror open via perception to the ten thousand things of Presence. So, once again: Ch'an's conceptual world as fundamentally Taoist in nature.

Ch'an sometimes also uses *mind* seemingly in the common English sense of the word, as the center of language and thought and memory, the mental apparatus of identity. It seems the same, but Taoist/Ch'an cosmology/ontology make it radically different. Those processes of mind were described as 意, which has a range of meanings: "intentionality," "desire," "meaning," "insight," "thought," "intelligence," "mind" (the faculty of thought). The natural Western assumption would be that these meanings refer exclusively to human consciousness, but 意 is also often used philosophically in describing the non-human world, as the "intentionality/desire/intelligence" that shapes the ongoing cosmological process of change and transformation (here it is virtually synonymous with *inner-pattern*). Each particular thing, at its very origin, has its own 意, as does the Cosmos as a whole. 意 can therefore be described as the "intentionality/intelligence/desire" infusing Absence (or Tao) and shaping its burgeoning forth into Presence, the ten thousand things of this Cosmos. It could also be described as the "intentionality," the inherent ordering capacity, shaping the creative force of *ch'i*.

This range of meaning links human intention/thought to the originary movements of the Cosmos—for it operates in a cosmological context recognizing an "intelligence" that infuses all existence, and of which human thought is but one manifestation. So, 意 is a capacity that human thought and emotion share with wild landscape and, indeed, the entire Cosmos, a reflection of the Chinese assumption that the human and non-human form a single tissue that "thinks" and "wants." Hence, thought/identity is not a transcendental spirit-realm separate from and looking out on reality, as we assume in the West. Instead, it is woven wholly into the ever-generative *ch'i*-tissue, into a living "intelligent" Cosmos—and so, it seems best translated as *ch'i*-weave mind, *ch'i*-weave insight, *ch'i*-weave thought, etc.

This concept appears perhaps most famously in the perennial Ch'an question: "What is the *ch'i*-weave mind Bodhidharma brought from the West?" This is said to be asking about the essence of Ch'an. Normal translations such as "purpose" or "meaning" cannot support such a claim—but once 意 is understood as "*ch'i*-weave mind," that claim makes sense, because then it's asking about mind woven into the generative tissue of the Cosmos. This is the heart of Ch'an understanding and enlightenment, and indeed one basis for the claim that we are always already enlightened.

EMPTY-MIND　空心, 虛心
NO-MIND　無心

The understanding of mind outlined above is the context within which we must understand one goal of Ch'an practice: to see through *mind* as the analytical faculty to *mind* as consciousness emptied of all contents. From this comes the terms *empty-mind* and *no-mind*—which are, confusingly, virtually synonymous with *mind* in its primary Ch'an sense. And they are central to Ch'an awakening, but awakening as more than the simple emptiness and tranquility of conventional Buddhism as it arrived in China.

For empty-mind was recognized as Absence itself, that generative cosmological/ontological tissue, source in consciousness of thought, memory, emotion, etc. And so, empty-mind was now dynamic and alive, an understanding emphasized in the etymological dimensions of 虛: "mountain tiger-sky," a poetic description of dynamic emptiness if there ever was one. And rather than an ascetic pursuit for a mind of tranquility and stillness, a state that is always forced and temporary (illusory!), Ch'an's Taoist assumptions allow an embrace of emptiness as the generative tissue of Absence, Tao, Cosmos. Hence, an acceptance of ordinary mind as always already awakened, always already Buddha, Tao, *tzu-jan*, *wu-wei*.

And it is the same for *no-mind*. Because of the ever-productive double meaning of 無 (no/Absence), 無心 (no-mind) describes mind both empty of content and made of the generative source-tissue (Absence-mind). It is accordingly here often translated "Absence no-mind." And so, again, an embrace of mind's processes as already awakened.

In ancient China, there was no fundamental distinction between heart and mind: 心 connotes all that we think of in the two concepts together. In fact, the ideogram is a stylized version of the earlier 心, which is an image of the heart muscle, with its chambers at the locus of veins and arteries. This integration of mental and emotional realms means the experience of empty- or no/Absence-mind cultivated in Ch'an practice is not just a spiritual or intellectual experience, but also a rich emotional experience.

EYE/SIGHT 目, 眼, 見, 直, ETC., MIRROR 鏡, 鑑

Once mind is emptied of all content (through meditation and sangha-case practice), the act of perception becomes a spiritual act: Absence no-mind mirror-deep, empty-mind mirroring the world, leaving its ten thousand things free of all thought and explanation—utterly simple, utterly themselves, and utterly sufficient. This image of the mirror is foundational in Taoism and Ch'an, recurring at key moments throughout the tradition. And it is the heart of Ch'an as a landscape practice. In such mirror-deep perception, earth's vast rivers-and-mountains landscape replaces thought and even identity itself, revealing the unity of consciousness/identity and landscape/Cosmos that is the heart of sage dwelling not only for Ch'an practitioners, but for all artist-intellectuals in ancient China. Indeed, when Buddha held up the flower and Mahakasyapa smiled, the understanding he revealed was exactly that: the mirror-deep seeing of empty-mind. And in the Ch'an tradition, Buddha describes that understanding "not relying on words and texts, outside teaching and beyond doctrine" as "my perfect dharma of the eye's treasure-house." This idea continued through the tradition as the essence of insight and awakening, for it encapsulates another way of meeting Buddha and all the patriarchs directly, but also of being indistinguishable from them, of being Buddha oneself.

AWAKENING/ENLIGHTENMENT 悟 / 見性

In Chinese, these two terms may seem quite different at the outset—but in the end, they describe the same awakening/enlightenment.

悟 (Japanese: *satori*) is composed etymologically of *mind* (心 appearing here in stylized form as 忄 on the left) and *me* (吾) on the right. This renders the term's common meaning of "waking" from sleep as a suddenly renewed awareness of "my mind," or perhaps "me" returning to "mind" again. And that becomes in the Ch'an context something very close to a "sudden awakening" (that essential Ch'an principle) to empty-mind as "original-nature." 見性 (Japanese: *kensho*) means "see + original-nature," where the ideogram for "original-nature" is composed of *mind* again on the left and *birth* on the right, hence "mind at its origin." This realization, an observational clarity almost scientific in nature, becomes the definition of enlightenment in the last line of Bodhidharma's seminal poem:

A separate transmission outside all teaching
and nowhere founded in eloquent scriptures,

it's simple: pointing directly at mind. There,
seeing original-nature, you become Buddha.

In spite of their apparent differences, the two terms both describe enlightenment as an awakening to oneself, to one's inherent or original-nature—and because that original-nature is whole and silent, prior to our mental machinery of words and concepts, awakening is instantaneous and outside of teaching and practice. That original-nature is unborn and empty, is in fact Way or Absence itself. And so, awakening/enlightenment is, again, a selfless "wandering boundless and free" through the selfless transformations of Way's vast and ongoing process.

For a full account of Ch'an awakening/enlightenment, see the Awakening chapter in my *China Root* (pp. 126–36).

Glossary of Buddhist Terms

BUDDHA 佛

Buddha refers most literally to Shakyamuni/Gautama, the historical Buddha, but also to a host of other Buddhas in Buddhist mythology. Beyond its use as an element of storytelling, Ch'an invests no faith in those mythologies. And it is primarily interested in Shakyamuni at the deep level of his essential nature, which is his empty-mind. So the meaning of the term *Buddha* expands to mean empty-mind, emphasized in the term *Buddha-nature*, and because empty-mind is the central concern of Ch'an, *Buddha* also came to mean the essence of Ch'an. Indeed, Ch'an's cultivation of empty-mind opens the possibility both of meeting the Buddha and the patriarchs directly, but also of being indistinguishable from them, of being Buddha oneself. And finally, as empty-mind is indistinguishable from Absence or dark-enigma, Buddha becomes synonymous with those terms too, and even the generative Way (Tao) itself. Hence, *Buddha* is absorbed into the Taoist cosmology, becoming another term used to describe that generative tissue that remains always just beyond language. Further, as we saw in the Introduction, the ideogram for *Buddha* is made up of the elements for "person" and "loom (of origins)." And from here, *Buddha* logically comes to mean reality itself—a usage we often find in the Ch'an tradition, and which has the effect of infusing our everyday world with a sense of the sacred. In particular, Buddha is identified with rivers-and-mountains landscape, as in Su Tung-p'o's enlightenment poem:

A murmuring stream is Buddha's tongue broad, unending,
and what is mountain color if not his body pure and clear?

BUDDHA EXISTENCE-TISSUE ARRIVAL 如來

Tathagata is a name for Buddha describing his nature as the "thus-come" or "thus perfected one." In its original Indian context, this would suggest an enlightened sage who has entered nirvana. In the Chinese transliteration, it means "existence-tissue arrival." Hence, Buddha has been transformed into a virtual equivalent of Way (Tao) or Absence—the generative "existence-tissue" (see Key Terms, p. 216) that is always, in its ongoing process of transformation, a moment of "arrival." Or alternately, as an enlightened sage who has "arrived" by inhabiting his original-nature as integral to the "existence-tissue."

DHARMA 法

Dharma in Ch'an can refer to the teachings of the Ch'an tradition. But Ch'an's essential teaching is outside of words and ideas, and here is *dharma*'s most fundamental meaning: the sheer thusness of things that is the true teaching. And this is actually the term's primary use in Ch'an—virtually synonymous with *tzu-jan*, *Tao*, *Absence* (*emptiness*), *dark-enigma*, even *Buddha*. Another example of a Buddhist term being adapted to function at the deepest cosmological/ontological levels of the Taoist conceptual world.

PRAJNA 慧, 般若

In Indian Buddhism, *prajna* refers to a transcendental state of perfect wisdom in which one directly sees or even becomes the fundamental emptiness (*sunyata*: see below) of things. Reconceived in the entirely empirical terms of Taoist cosmology/ontology, it is defined in a host of related ways in the Ch'an tradition, but a good working definition is mind returned to its original-nature as "Absence," which is equated with empty-mind as a "dark-enigma mirror." This reveals a profound shift from Sanskrit/Buddhism to Chinese/Ch'an, for *prajna* has been reconfigured into a Taoist concept. Again, metaphysics replaced by the great transformation itself: this wild earth we inhabit.

SAMADHI 三昧地

In the *dhyana* Buddhism that migrated to China from India, *samadhi* simply meant "consciousness emptied of all subjective content," the goal of meditative practice. But its Chinese transliteration means "three-shadowed earth." And so, *dhyana*'s abstract and cerebral meditative state has been invested with the earthly dimensions of Taoism/Ch'an: empty-mind free of all conceptual structures, self dismantled completely by the Ch'an wrecking-crew, leaving consciousness open to its "original-nature" as the Cosmos moving in perfect tranquility at that all-encompassing and perennial origin-place that Lao Tzu called *Absence*. In its consummate description of enlightenment, *No-Gate Gateway* declares that in awakening "you wander the playfulness of *samadhi*'s three-shadowed earth."

SAMSARA 輪迴

Samsara's traditional Buddhist meaning is "the illusory universe we inhabit as we work out our karmic destiny," a meaning sometimes referenced derisively in Ch'an. Generally though, *samsara* refers in Ch'an to the phenomenal universe of our everyday experience.

SUNYATA 空, 虛

In its original Indian Buddhist context, *sunyata* means "emptiness"—but "emptiness" in the sense that things have no intrinsic nature or self-existence, that they are illusory or delusions conjured by the mind. Here, it is closely associated with *nirvana* as a state of selfless and transcendental extinction or *emptiness*. This *sunyata* emptiness is essentially metaphysical, suggesting some kind of "ultimate reality" behind or beyond the physical world we inhabit. But this atmosphere of metaphysics is quite foreign to the Chinese sensibility and Ch'an. Indeed, there was no word in Chinese with the meaning of *sunyata*. 空 and 虛 (*emptiness*: see Key Terms, p. 222), with their superficial similarities, were quite simply the only possibility. And in the Taoist context, *emptiness* is virtually synonymous with *Absence*, reality seen as a single formless and generative tissue that is the source of all things—a concept altogether different from the

Buddhist *sunyata*. Translation and interpretation of Ch'an in modern America often treats 空 and 虛 as *sunyata*—but in the Chinese, the term has lost its Sanskrit meaning, replacing it with the native Chinese one. Indeed, this reinvention of *sunyata* as 空 and 虛 was a defining moment in the creation of Ch'an.

Index to Ch'an Figures

1. English Names with Chinese Equivalents

ENGLISH	WADE-GILES	PINYIN	SANGHA-CASE
Absence-Belong	Wu Chu	Wu Zhu	35
Bodhidharma	P'u T'i Ta Mo	Pu Ti Da Mo	1, passim
Cinnabar-Cloud Mountain	Tan Hsia	Dan Xia	76
Clarity-Mirror Mountain	Ching Ch'ing	Jing Qing	16, 23, 46
Cloud-Crag Mountain	Yün Yen	Yun Yan	70, 72, 89
Cloud-Gate Mountain	Yün Men	Yun Men	6, 8, 14, 15, 22, 27, 34, 39, 47, 50, 54, 60, 62, 77, 83, 86, 87, 88
Crag-Summit Mountain	Yen T'ou	Yan Tou	51, 66
Dark-Enigma-Sands Mountain	Hsüan Sha	Xuan Sha	22, 56, 88
Dharma-Eye	Fa Yen	Fa Yan	7
Dice-Thrown Mountain	T'ou Tzu	Tou Zi	41, 79, 80, 91
Dragon-Fang Mountain	Lung Ya	Long Ya	20
Fathom Mountain	Tung Shan (Liang Chieh)	Dong Shan (Liang Jie)	20, 43
Fathom Mountain	Tung Shan (Shou Chu)	Dong Shan (Shou Zhu)	12
Field-Grain Mountain	Ho Shan	He Shan	44
Five-Peak Mountain	Wu Feng	Wu Feng	70, 71
Flax-Canyon Mountain	Ma Ku	Ma Gu	31, 69
Flood-Deva Risen	T'i P'o	Ti Po	13
Heart-Sight Mountain	Te Shan (Hsüan Chien)	De Shan (Xuan Jian)	4

English	Wade-Giles	Pinyin	Sangha-Case
Samadhi-Still Land	Ting Chou	Ding Zhou	32, 75
Shelter-Dragon Layman	P'ang Chü-Shih	Pang Ju-Shih	42
Snow-Chute Mountain	Hsüeh Tou	Xue Dou	1–100
Snow-Peak Mountain	Hsüeh Feng	Xue Feng	5, 22, 44, 49, 51, 66
Source-Ancestral Return	Kuei Tsung	Gui Zong	69
Stone-Frost Mountain	Shih Shuang	Shi Shuang	55, 91
Three-Sage Mountain	San Sheng	San Sheng	49, 68
Tumble-Vast Mountain	Ta Sui	Da Sui	29
Vimalakirti	Wei Mo Chieh	Wei Mo Jie	84
Visitation-Land	Chao Chou	Zhao Zhou	2, 9, 30, 41, 45, 52, 57, 58, 59, 64, 80, 96
Way-I Mountain	Tao Wu	Dao Wu	55, 89
Wellspring-South Mountain	Nan Ch'üan	Nan Quan	28, 30, 31, 40, 63, 64, 69
Wind-Source Mountain	Feng Hsüeh	Feng Xue	38, 61
Wisdom-Gate Mountain	Chih Men	Zhi Men	21, 90
Wisdom-Hoard	Chih Tsang	Zhi Zang	73
Yellow-Bitterroot Mountain	Huang Po	Huang Bo	11, 32

2. Chinese Names with English Equivalents

Wade-Giles	Pinyin	English	Sangha-Case
Nan Ch'üan	Nan Quan	Wellspring-South Mountain	28, 30, 31, 40, 63, 64, 69
Nan-Yang Hui-Chung	Nan-Yang Hui-Zhong	Prajna-Devotion	18, 69, 99
Pa Ling	Ba Ling	Open-Hand Ridge	13, 100
P'ang Chü-Shih	Pang Ju-Shih	Shelter-Dragon Layman	42
Pao Chih	Bao Zhi	Remembrance-Treasure	1, 67
Pao Fu	Bao Fu	Prosper-Nurture Mountain	8, 23, 76, 91, 95
Po (Pai) Chang	Bai Zhang	Hundred-Elder Mountain	26, 28, 53, 70, 71, 72, 73
P'o Tsao-To	Po Zao-Duo	Oven-Smasher	96
P'u T'i Ta Mo	Pu-Ti Da-Mo	Bodhidharma	1, passim
San Sheng	San Sheng	Three-Sage Mountain	49, 68
Shih Shuang	Shi Shuang	Stone-Forest Mountain	55, 91
Ta Kuang	Dao Guang	Lumen-Vast Mountain	93
Ta Sui	Da Sui	Tumble-Vast Mountain	29
Tan Hsia	Dan Xia	Cinnabar-Cloud Mountain	76
Tao Wu	Dao Wu	Way-I Mountain	55, 89
Te Shan (Hsüan Chien)	De Shan (Xuan Jian)	Heart-Sight Mountain	4
T'i P'o	Ti Po	Flood-Deva Risen	13
T'ieh Mo	Tie Mo	Iron-Grinder	17, 24
Ting Chou	Ding Zhou	Samadhi-Still Land	32, 75
T'ou Tzu	Tou Zi	Dice-Thrown Mountain	41, 79, 80, 91
Ts'ui Wei	Cui Wei	Kingfisher Shadowed-Emergence	20
Ts'ui Yen	Cui Yan	Kingfisher-Cliff Mountain	8
Tung Shan (Liang Chieh)	Dong Shan (Liang Jie)	Fathom Mountain	20, 43
Tung Shan (Shou Chu)	Dong Shan (Shou Zhu)	Fathom Mountain	12
Tzu Fu	Zi Fu	Prosper-Sustain Mountain	33, 91
Tzu Hu	Zi Hu	Mongrol Purple-Calm	17, 96

Wade-Giles	Pinyin	English	Sangha-Case
Wei Mo-Chieh	Wei Mo-Jie	Vimalakirti	84
Wen Shu	Wen Shu	Manjusri	35, 84, 92
Wu Chiu	Wu Jiu	Night-Crow Mountain	75
Wu Chu	Wu Zhu	Absence-Belong	35
Wu Feng	Wu Feng	Five-Peak Mountain	70, 71
Yang Shan	Yang Shan	Reliance Mountain	34, 68
Yao Shan	Yao Shan	Medicine Mountain	42, 81
Yen Kuan	Yan Guan	Salt-Legal Mountain	91
Yen T'ou	Yan Tou	Crag-Summit Mountain	51, 66
Yün Men	Yun Men	Cloud-Gate Mountain	6, 8, 14, 15, 22, 27, 34, 39, 47, 50, 54, 60, 62, 77, 83, 86, 87, 88
Yün Yen	Yun Yan	Cloud-Crag Mountain	70, 72, 89

Sangha-Cases Included in Other Collections

BLUE-CLIFF RECORD (CA. 1040 C.E.)	CAREFREE-EASE RECORD (CA. 1145)	NO-GATE GATEWAY (1228)
1	2	
2	36	
3		
4		
5		
6		
7		
8	71	
9		
10		
11	53	
12		18
13		
14		
15		
16		
17		
18	85	
19	84	3
20	80	
21		
22	24	
23		

BLUE-CLIFF RECORD (CA. 1040 C.E.)	CAREFREE-EASE RECORD (CA. 1145)	NO-GATE GATEWAY (1228)
24	60	
25		
26		
27		
28		27
29	30	
30		
31	16	
32		
33		
34		
35		
36		
37		
38	29	
39		
40	91	
41	63	
42		
43		
44		
45		
46		
47		
48		
49	33	
50	99	
51	50	
52		
53		

BLUE-CLIFF RECORD (CA. 1040 C.E.)	CAREFREE-EASE RECORD (CA. 1145)	NO-GATE GATEWAY (1228)
54		
55		
56		
57		
58		
59		
60		
61	34	
62	92	
63	9	14
64	9	14
65		32
66		
67		
68		
69		
70		
71		
72		
73	6	
74		
75		
76		
77	78	
78		
79		
80		
81		
82		
83	31	

BLUE-CLIFF RECORD (CA. 1040 C.E.)	CAREFREE-EASE RECORD (CA. 1145)	NO-GATE GATEWAY (1228)
84	48	
85		
86		
87		
88		
89	54	
90		
91	25	
92	1	
93		
94	88	
95		
96		
97	58	
98		
99		
100